Product Safety Excellence

Product Safety Excellence

The Seven Elements Essential for Product Liability Prevention

Timothy A. Pine

ASQ Quality Press
Milwaukee, Wisconsin

American Society for Quality, Quality Press, Milwaukee 53203
© 2012 by ASQ
All rights reserved.
Printed in the United States of America
17 16 15 14 13 12   5 4 3 2 1

Library of Congress Cataloging-in-Publication Data

Pine, Timothy A., 1949–
    Product safety excellence : the seven elements essential for
product liability prevention / Timothy A. Pine.
        p. cm.
    ISBN 978-0-87389-842-3 (alk. paper)
    1. Product safety.   2. Product design.   3. Consumer protection.
4. Products liability.   I. Title.
    TS175.P56 2012
    363.19—dc23

                                                    2012013749

Publisher: William A. Tony
Acquisitions Editor: Matt Meinholz
Project Editor: Paul Daniel O'Mara
Production Administrator: Randall Benson

ASQ Mission: The American Society for Quality advances individual, organizational, and community excellence worldwide through learning, quality improvement, and knowledge exchange.

Attention Bookstores, Wholesalers, Schools, and Corporations: ASQ Quality Press
books, video, audio, and software are available at quantity discounts with bulk
purchases for business, educational, or instructional use. For information, please
contact ASQ Quality Press at 800-248-1946, or write to ASQ Quality Press,
P.O. Box 3005, Milwaukee, WI 53201-3005.

To place orders or to request a free copy of the ASQ Quality Press Publications
Catalog, visit our website at http://www.asq.org/quality-press.

∞ Printed on acid-free paper

Quality Press
600 N. Plankinton Ave.
Milwaukee, WI 53203-2914
E-mail: authors@asq.org

ASQ® **The Global Voice of Quality™**

To Pat, a remarkable and lovely wife, friend, patriot, Christian, and mother of our children.

Contents

List of Figures

Preface

Product safety problems are very damaging to companies, their names, and their brands. They cause injuries, lawsuits, recalls, penalties, complaints, returns, schedule delays, scrap, and rework. They waste company resources, alienate consumers, frustrate employees, and leave company stakeholders disgusted.

It is easy to understand why most consumer product companies are committed to product safety and why they often seem willing to devote even more resources to increase their organization's safety commitment. Their logic seems to be that this kind of action will result in higher levels of safety performance.

Achieving excellence in product safety is not about seeking more commitment. Most organizations are already very committed to product safety—just ask them. Achieving product safety excellence is all about understanding what to do and how to do it using the fine organization one already has.

Product Safety Excellence defines the seven vital elements that are essential for achieving excellence in product safety, and it describes the tools and processes that make up each element. The application of these seven elements will provide a proven system for state-of-the-art consumer product safety performance with the benefits of product liability prevention, product quality improvement, and higher levels of consumer trust and loyalty.

This book is appropriate for anyone interested in under-standing the concepts underlying product safety excellence. It should especially be read by management and technical per-sonnel with a responsibility and/or desire for eliminating prod-uct safety problems and improving profitability and consumer loyalty. I have attempted to make *Product Safety Excellence* concise, clear, and easy to read by anyone with some general business experience or knowledge.

My sincere hope and prayer is that this book will help guide and inspire individuals and organizations toward higher levels of performance and state-of-the-art product safety.

Acknowledgments

So whoever knows the right thing to do and fails to do it,
for him it is sin.

—JAMES 4:17 ESV

Product safety information and best practices are really meant to be shared within companies, between companies, and between industries. Promoting safety with this type of sharing is a responsibility of all companies. It is recognized that if one company has a serious product safety failure, it adversely affects, to some extent, all companies in that industry. Sharing best practices, therefore, benefits all companies.

I am truly thankful and appreciative for all of the great companies I have either worked for or been affiliated with that have strongly supported benchmarking and the sharing of information for the purpose of advancing product safety. I am even more thankful for the opportunity to have worked directly with so many excellent individuals to achieve, support, and advance product safety initiatives. There are several in particular whom I must name because of their outstanding support and contributions: Kathrin Belliveau, Sandra Biets, Marty Cahill, KS Chan, Ken Collins, Scott Crump, Sean Flanagan, Joe Fortino, Jenny Foster, Jim Hanners, Lindsay Harris, Denis Hogya, William Ip, Ron Jackson, Gary Jones, Jerry Karver, Jill Kashiwagi,

Arthur Kazianis, Jim Kipling, John Kraus, Mary Kuo, Dave Mauer, Joe Mendelsohn, Kitty Pilarz, Bill Quinlan, Gerry Remmy, Terri Rogers, Tim Schuh, Daryl Scrivens, Vincent Tam, KL Tsui, Chris Vacca, Fred Virrazzi, Karl Wojahn, and CK Wong.

I especially want to thank Gary Jones, a close friend and highly respected longtime associate, for providing valuable and insightful comments on the first draft.

I must also thank Karl Wojahn in particular for the abundance of education, training, mentoring, encouragement, and support he provided me throughout my career. Without it, I never would have been able to write this book.

And finally, a special thank-you goes to Pat Pine, my loving wife, confidante, and life partner, for conscientiously and thoroughly reviewing early drafts and providing brilliant critiques when I know she would have much rather been reading entirely different and less technical material.

My sincere thanks go to all of you.

Timothy A. Pine
March 2012

1

Introduction

In all things, the supreme excellence is simplicity.

—HENRY WADSWORTH LONGFELLOW

Effective product safety management is really all about preventing errors. This means focusing on product and process design, understanding consumer behavior with respect to product use and misuse, applying human factors, performing thorough risk assessments, and maintaining an awareness of emerging hazards and diverse medical and technical information. It is not about just meeting mandatory and voluntary standards, product testing to these standards, inspecting product, or adding lots of warnings. This book defines what product safety excellence is all about and describes how to apply the appropriate tools and processes to achieve it.

EXCELLENCE VS. PERFECTION

There is no such thing as a perfectly safe product. In product safety, perfection is just not possible. Virtually anything can be unsafe or hazardous if it is misused or abused. A bucket of water can be a drowning hazard to a top-heavy toddler who leans over to look inside the bucket. A grape has been known to cause choking fatalities in young children. Even a crayon can easily break into small parts that can create an asphyxiation hazard to children. Clearly, it is impossible to eliminate *all* hazards from any product.

Hazard

A *hazard* is defined as a potential source of harm. Harm can be personal injury and/or property damage. Hazards can range from the relatively minor (e.g., a sharp point) to the very severe (e.g., high toxicity or electrocution). Hazards can also range from a relatively low-exposure "inaccessible" to a relatively high-exposure 100% accessible. For example, an exposed 115-volt (household current) metal part presents a severe hazard if the exposure is high; that is, it is readily accessible to the touch or incidental contact. This same metal part contained within the insulated housing of a toy oven presents the same severe hazard but with a very low, inaccessible exposure. Although the hazard is the same whether the 115-volt part is accessible or inaccessible, the risk of injury is clearly not the same.

Risk

The term *risk* is used to express the combination of hazard severity and hazard exposure (probability of harm). Risk is the product of "probability of harm" and "severity of that harm." Risk is the most appropriate measure of product safety because it includes both exposure and severity factors.

Safety

Safety is defined as freedom from unacceptable risk. It is not defined as freedom from risk, because just as not all hazards can be eliminated, not all risk can be eliminated. It therefore follows that safety is also not defined as freedom from hazards. Since unacceptable risk is considered to be unreasonable risk, safety is also defined as freedom from unreasonable risk.

Unreasonable Risk

A product is unsafe if it presents an unreasonable risk of harm to the consumer. This means that the product must be designed for reasonably foreseeable use and misuse by the user. Sometimes there are mandatory and industry safety standards that define tests for reasonably foreseeable abuse. The manufacturer may need to consider human factors and perform surveys and human test trials to obtain information on *reasonably foreseeable use and misuse*, which can be defined as conduct expected of a reasonably prudent person.

Reasonable risk is a fact of life, and a reasonably safe product is never expected to be an absolutely safe one. If the product use that causes an injury is not reasonably foreseeable, then no negligence or product liability exists. The following are some considerations that could establish whether the risk is reasonable/acceptable:

1. The usefulness and desirability of the product taking into account economic and social benefits and costs (e.g., automobiles)

2. The obviousness of the danger (e.g., knives)

3. The unavailability of other, safer products that would meet the same needs (e.g., X-ray machines)

4. The avoidability of injury by reasonable care in the use of the product (e.g., lawnmowers)

5. Common knowledge and normal public expectation of the danger (e.g., home electrical outlets)

Manufacturers are not responsible for a hazard that's scientifically unknowable at the time of manufacture. As technology changes, new hazards emerge and it is not expected or even possible that they be addressed retroactively. It is, however, expected that manufacturers will meet the state-of-the-art technology and standards for product safety that exist at the time of manufacture.

State of the Art

State of the art means the level of technical knowledge and standards that exist at the time of product creation. A manufacturer must have and keep the systems, resources, and leadership in place to maintain a product safety program that is state of the art. Anything less than this level will put the manufacturer in jeopardy of major losses in sales, profits, customers, and brand value.

Perfection is not expected or even possible in product safety. Excellence, however, is both possible and expected. It is achieved by maintaining a state-of-the-art product safety process.

INVEST IN PREVENTION

The only way to achieve excellence in product safety is to prevent defects from occurring in the first place. Prevention means successfully applying appropriate tools and processes to eliminate opportunities for the occurrence of defects, errors, and waste. It is much more effective and much less costly to prevent defects than it is to try to find them and eliminate them after they occur. In fact, it is virtually impossible to eliminate all defects once they are inherent in the product design and manufacturing process. They must be prevented.

The earlier in the product development process that defects are prevented, the easier and less costly it is. It is clearly much easier and faster to alter sketches and drawings than it is to change tooling and equipment. It can also be quite disconcerting to a product development team to find out late in the development cycle that there is a design flaw that should have been discovered and addressed much earlier. And the longer it takes to discover a design flaw, the greater the damage to the company. The investment in prevention activities must begin at the earliest stages of product concept review, before there is a significant investment in time, expense, and emotion.

DESIGN DEFECTS AND RECALLS

The majority of Consumer Product Safety Commission (CPSC) recalls and injuries in the past decade were a result of *design* defects. A design defect is particularly troubling—more so than a manufacturing defect—because it generally affects 100% of the products produced and shipped, so the exposure (probability of harm) is high. This highlights the importance of thorough design reviews and assessments.

VOLUNTARY AND REGULATORY REQUIREMENTS AND RECALLS

The majority of CPSC recalls in the past decade involved product that met the voluntary and regulatory requirements. This highlights the importance of using comprehensive design assessments that go far beyond just ensuring that basic published safety standards are met. Achieving product safety excellence is much more than just meeting generic safety standards. It is indeed important to meet all voluntary and regulatory requirements, but, as noted earlier, that is often not nearly enough.

Product design assessments must also include such things as using hazard identification checklists, reviewing general injury information, understanding human factors, and evaluating foreseeable product use and misuse. These tools and more will be covered in the next few chapters.

COMPREHENSION VS. COMMITMENT

Achieving product safety excellence is not about getting more worker commitment. If it were, then practically everyone would already be achieving excellence. Most organizations are already very committed to product safety. Achieving product safety excellence is about comprehension. It is about understanding what to do and how to do it. It is about educating the organization to understand and apply the right tools and processes. It is about enabling the organization with comprehension, not pushing it for more commitment.

There are seven vital elements that make up a comprehensive product safety program. With all seven elements in place, a business can achieve excellence in product safety, with resulting improvements in costs, schedules, profitability, and consumer trust and loyalty.

THE SEVEN VITAL ELEMENTS

The key to achieving product safety excellence can be reduced to just seven necessary elements. These seven elements, each covered in a separate chapter, are as follows:

- *Technical collaboration*—Using knowledge resources

- *Concept evaluation*—Achieving inherently safe designs

- *Design qualification*—Confirming safety, reliability, and manufacturability

- *Supplier qualification*—Verifying capabilities, capacities, controls, and commitment

- *Product qualification*—Documenting design and process and testing conformance

- *Supplier quality process*—Verifying process performance

- *Strategic auditing*—Monitoring, confirming, and improving effectiveness of prevention systems

Figure 1.1 shows the basic product safety process of the seven vital elements. Each chapter has been constructed to concisely define each element and to focus on the key topics that describe each one. The idea is to provide a simple, clear, and concise

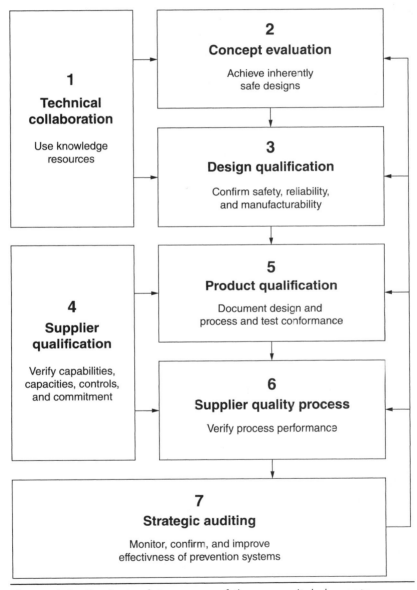

Figure 1.1   Product safety process of the seven vital elements.

road map to facilitate a complete understanding of a comprehensive product safety process. The application of these seven elements will enable the achievement of product safety excellence. If, however, even one of the elements is missing or inadequate, success is jeopardized, and defects, waste, and product liability become significant problems.

To facilitate a good comprehension of these seven critical elements, every attempt has been made to keep the presentations and discussions as simple and relevant as possible. As Longfellow noted, simplicity is the supreme excellence.

2

Technical Collaboration

Using Knowledge Resources

A manager is responsible for the application and performance of knowledge.

—PETER DRUCKER

Lack of knowledge is a major root cause of product safety errors. For each new product concept there is a body of knowledge that is required to ensure a thorough safety assessment. The problem is that some of this required knowledge can be highly specialized and quite esoteric, and the product safety engineer and the manager can be completely unaware of it. Therefore, *technical collaboration*—the communication and information exchange with the outside network of knowledge resources—is necessary when dealing with new and unusual product concepts.

DISCOVERING NEEDED KNOWLEDGE

The knowledge required for a comprehensive safety assessment may include some things that you know about and some things that you don't know about. The things you already know about are generally not areas where product safety problems arise, providing, of course, that lack of attention is not an issue. The things that you don't know about are the areas of concern.

The things that you *know* you don't know about aren't usually a problem area. In these situations you are at least aware that expert assistance is required. When you know that you need help, you generally know where to find it or at least how to go about finding it.

The things that you *don't know* you don't know about are the big troublemakers. Figure 2.1 shows this graphically. In these situations it is very easy to think that you have addressed all the issues and to proceed full speed ahead with blind ignorance. After all, how can you ask for help when you don't even know that you need it?

This is why maintaining a technical collaboration network is such an important product safety process element. Innovative companies are often involved with new product concepts that use new technologies, materials, and manufacturing methods, and this often requires having access to a wide range of technical expertise. Trying to maintain all of this diverse expertise within the company's organization would be inefficient and cost prohibitive. It can be much more cost effective to augment the company organization with outside technical and product safety resources that are available when needed.

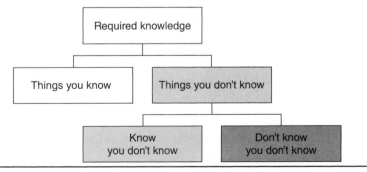

Figure 2.1   Knowing what you do know and don't know.

As Peter Drucker noted, company management is responsible for the application and performance of knowledge. This chapter presents examples of resources that are available for technical collaboration to ensure that needed knowledge is readily acquired.

NEISS INFORMATION

The National Electronic Injury Surveillance System (NEISS) is an injury data collection system operated by the CPSC. Its primary purpose is to collect data on consumer product–related injuries occurring in the United States. A sample of approximately 100 hospital emergency departments enables the CPSC to make national estimates of injuries *associated* with (not necessarily caused by) specific consumer products. The data are used by the CPSC for setting priorities for the following:

• Development of new product safety standards

• Product recall determinations

• Public awareness campaigns

• Further study

The NEISS information is an important product safety research tool that is available to the public at http://www.cpsc.gov/library/neiss.html. Click on "Query NEISS" at the bottom of the page; enter the product code, year desired, and other parameters, if needed; and click on "Submit Query" for the CPSC injury data. Product codes are available at http://www.cpsc.gov/neiss/completemanual.pdf.

The information provided by NEISS can be very valuable when considering expanding your product line into new product areas. Using historical product injury information may prevent similar injury experiences from occurring with your new products.

CPSC RECALL HISTORY

The CPSC has jurisdiction over more than 15,000 categories of consumer products used in and around the home, in sports, in recreation, and in schools. Information on over 5000 product recalls and recall alerts since 1973 can be found using the following CPSC website: http://www.cpsc.gov/cpscpub/prerel/prerel.html. Searches can be made by month and year, product type, company, and hazard.

When evaluating and assessing potential new product categories, a review of product recall information for similar products can be very beneficial and can help prevent you from making the same or similar mistakes that other manufacturers made with their recalled products. A comprehensive product safety process uses product recall information as one part of a complete review of new product concepts.

TRADE ASSOCIATIONS

A *trade association* is an organization of businesses that operate in a specific industry. A main focus of many trade associations is collaboration between member companies for industry standardization, especially industry product safety standards. Some examples of trade associations that are active in product safety standards are the Juvenile Products Manufacturers Association (JPMA), the American Association of Textile Chemists and Colorists (AATCC), the Association of Home Appliance Manufacturers (AHAM), and the Toy Industry Association (TIA).

The TIA is very active in establishing, implementing, and maintaining uniform risk-based national safety standards. The TIA has a Safety Standards and Technical Committee (SSTC) made up of representatives from toy manufacturers and toy retailers who continually review industry and CPSC data for the purpose of ensuring that the industry safety standard is kept up to date. TIA representatives also work on the ASTM International

Toy Safety committee, along with consumer representatives, test laboratories, and CPSC representatives, to maintain the industry toy safety standard known as ASTM F963.

A benefit of working on trade association safety committees is keeping current with the latest safety standards and the rationales behind the standards. The rationale for each safety standard provides information on how and why the standard was developed, which is important for ensuring that the standard is fully understood and correctly applied to products.

Another significant benefit of trade association safety committee work is obtaining early firsthand knowledge of emerging hazards. Advances in technology can lead to unintended negative consequences in the form of emerging hazards. For example, with the emergence of very powerful rare earth magnets came a new type of hazard. The rare earth magnets were so powerful that they could be made small enough to fit into small toys. The problem was that the small magnets could be swallowed, creating a very serious problem for the digestive system. The swallowed magnets could be strongly attracted to each other even through the intestinal walls. This attraction could pinch the intestines, creating perforations that could result in very serious infections. The old ferrous magnets were too weak to create this hazard.

It should be noted that as a result of this new information, the toy industry safety standard was immediately revised to restrict the accessibility of any small powerful magnets in toys.

Technical collaboration with trade associations can provide important safety knowledge on safety standards. Most importantly, it can also provide critical information on standard rationales and emerging hazards.

MEDICAL EXPERTISE AND ACADEMIA

Having direct access to medical specialists at local hospitals and to professors at local universities to supplement your organization can be very important when evaluating new product concepts for safety. This is especially true if the new products will be using new material formulations that could present concerns relating to toxicity, eye or skin irritation, allergenicity, or similar hazards.

The Labeling of Hazardous Art Materials Act (LHAMA) applies to products such as crayons, chalk, pencils, paint sets, modeling clay, and any other products used by children to produce a work of visual art. The law requires that all such art materials be reviewed by a board-certified toxicologist to determine the potential for causing a chronic hazard. In this case, toxicological expertise is mandatory.

Products that could be considered projectiles may require the expertise of an ophthalmologist during safety assessment. Products that emit intense light may require the expertise of a medical professional during an assessment of light toxicity. When there are new product concepts to evaluate, a comprehensive safety review can require outside medical expertise.

LABORATORIES AND CONSULTING FIRMS

A good source of product safety information is one of the international testing laboratories. These laboratories generally have technical staff members who serve on industry safety committees that assist in the development and maintenance of industry safety standards. This activity keeps the laboratories well versed in new industry standards and, just as important, the rationales behind the standards.

The international laboratories generally have a very diverse technical staff with specialists in different product areas. They also have substantial testing experience with a broad array of different products. These resources can provide useful interpretations and explanations of safety requirements and test procedures. These laboratories are generally widely certified, even by the CPSC.

Engineering, risk analysis, and other product safety consulting firms are available for issues that go beyond the skill sets of the test laboratories. Having direct access to consulting firms and international testing laboratories should be a significant part of any firm's technical collaboration network.

PARTNER SUPPLIER INPUT

For maximum success in the twenty-first century, it is important to develop strategic partnerships with your top, key suppliers. A *strategic partnership* is a commitment by both the supplier and the customer (your company) to a long-term relationship involving joint business planning and a sharing of strategies, costs, and technology. The supplier becomes an extension of your company, and you ensure a stable order flow to your partner supplier. You and your partner supplier collaborate on innovations and provide active, concrete help to each other. It is a relationship of mutual trust, high ethics, uncompromising integrity, and transparency. Compatible values and a strong ethical foundation are essential criteria for selecting a partner supplier.

It is prudent to include the voice of your strategic partner suppliers in your new product design review process. The manufacturing perspective and input of a partner supplier can help ensure the manufacturability of new designs. Their manufacturing experience and expertise can help simplify designs for ease of manufacture to reduce labor and quality costs. Early collaboration with partner suppliers will help you to be more knowledgeable and circumspect in the quest for product safety excellence.

BENCHMARKING AND COMPETITION

It can be beneficial to routinely meet with best-in-class companies to search for new ideas, processes, methods, and best practices. The constant search for best practices must draw from a broad range of industries, since methods used in other industries can often be valuable to your organization. Seeing what other industries are doing to build consumer loyalty and achieve competitive advantage can be very instructive.

The benchmarking activity involves touring the company's operation and sharing information to fully understand its systems, processes, and methodologies. This is particularly important in the area of product safety. Sharing this type of information benefits both companies and most importantly the consumer. Benchmarking helps a company keep current with state-of-the-art product safety technology, processes, and standards.

It is also beneficial to routinely test and evaluate the product of your major competition. It is acknowledged that the primary focus must be on the consumer and not on the competition. From a product safety standpoint, however, it can be beneficial to know what the competition is doing with respect to product design and quality, reliability, and safety performance. Competitive product evaluation is just another step in the journey of maintaining state-of-the-art knowledge with respect to product safety.

SUMMARY

Technical collaboration is using knowledge resources to discover the knowledge required to properly execute a new product concept. Major knowledge resources include CPSC NEISS and recall information, trade associations, medical experts and academia, certified laboratories and consultants, partner suppliers, and benchmarking and competition activities. These resource tools can help ensure thorough and comprehensive evaluations of new product concepts—evaluations that will keep your products and processes state of the art with respect to product safety.

3

Concept Evaluation
Achieving Inherently Safe Designs

True genius resides in the capacity for evaluation of uncertain, hazardous, and conflicting information.

—WINSTON CHURCHILL

*C*oncept evaluation, the earliest stage of product design and development, occurs when the product is only an idea or a general concept. The product is initially defined by sketches and maybe brief descriptions of what the product is and does. It is at this stage that the product is most conducive to change and correction for having safety designed into it. It is very important to thoroughly evaluate and influence product concepts early in the process rather than waiting and trying to do it at a later stage of development.

EARLY SAFETY INFLUENCE

Since the objective is to make the product inherently safe, there is no better opportunity to do this than at the concept stage, where changes are the easiest to implement. If opportunities for safety influence are missed at the concept stage, then they would need to happen at a later stage of development, when more time, dollars, and effort would need to be invested. It becomes more and more difficult and costly to ensure inherently safe products as the concept moves further and further through the product development process. Over time the organization becomes more and more attached to a product, and any efforts to make late changes may be met with objections because of lead time, delivery, cost, and emotional product-attachment issues. This can lead to compromises that would not have been necessary if the changes had occurred at the early concept stage.

There is a downside to investing resources at the concept stage of development. It is not unusual for product concepts to be dropped from the product line because they end up not being viable. The time and resources invested in these product concepts are lost. This loss, however, is a small price to pay for the huge benefit realized on the investment in early safety influence for those product concepts that do make it in the product line. *Product safety resources must be invested in every new product concept, regardless of its eventual fate.*

HAZARD IDENTIFICATION CHECKLISTS

A design concept evaluation generally begins with the identification and evaluation of potential hazards. To ensure that a design concept is thoroughly evaluated for potential hazards, a hazard identification checklist must be used. A list of generic hazard categories that should be considered in developing a hazard evaluation checklist is shown in Figure 3.1. This checklist tool should be constructed and continually upgraded as

Mechanical	Flammability	Microbiological
Pinch/Amputation	Solids/Textiles	Bacteria/Virus
Crushing	Liquids	Yeast/Mold
Shearing	Gases	Preservative efficacy
Laceration	Mists/Dusts	Filth and contamination
Puncture		
Projectiles	**Thermal**	**Human factors**
Abrasion	Hot surfaces	Strength
Friction	Cold surfaces	Stamina
Insertion	Expansion	Reaction time
Entanglement	Contraction	Human error
Entrapment	Decomposition	Stress
Stability		Cognitive overload
Overload	**Electrical**	Perception
Small parts/Choking	Shock	
Aspiration	Overcurrent/Fires	**Control**
Magnets/Ingestion	Sparks/Arcs	Inadvertent activation
Strangulation	Batteries	Failure to activate
Suction		Inadequate visibility
Drowning	**Toxicity**	Ambiguity
	Oral	Emergency off
Falls	Dermal	
From elevation	Inhalation	**Environment**
Slips	Light	High temperature
Trips	Carcinogenic	Low temperature
Uneven surfaces	Allergenicity	Humidity/Rain
Falling over		Ozone
Falling onto	**Irritation**	Ultraviolet radiation
Falling with	Eye	Sand/Dust
	Skin sensitization	Vacuum
Noise	Corrosion	Lightning
Continuous		Fog
Impulsive	**Radiation**	
	Ultraviolet	
	Infrared	
	Laser	

Figure 3.1 List of generic hazard categories.

new information becomes available and new product experiences occur.

Information from mandatory and industry safety standards and their rationales should also be factored into the hazard identification checklist. Proposed standards for product safety and emerging hazards information should likewise be incorporated into the checklist. It is also important to include information acquired from the technical collaboration activities. The hazard identification checklist, therefore, is a living and evolving tool that serves to ensure that thorough evaluations occur for all potential hazards.

ENERGY-HAZARD RELATIONSHIP

It can generally be stated that all products become hazardous upon the transfer of energy in excessive amounts. This includes both kinetic energy and potential energy. The *kinetic energy* of a product or component is the energy it has due to its motion. This includes such objects as projectiles, powered gear trains, and propellers. The *potential energy* of a product is the energy stored in the product or due to the position of the product. This includes such objects as batteries in products, loaded spring mechanisms, pressurized containers, or even positioning the product on an elevated surface (where it could subsequently fall).

In concert with the use of hazard identification checklists, new product concepts must be evaluated for all accessible or potentially accessible sources of energy. These sources of energy can fall under the same hazard categories as those listed in Figure 3.1.

FORESEEABLE USE AND MISUSE

It is not enough that a product be free of unacceptable hazards when the consumer receives it. The product must also remain safe (free from unreasonable risks) when it is subjected to reasonably foreseeable use and misuse, which includes reasonably foreseeable damage or abuse. Any new product concept evaluation, therefore, must include an assessment of reasonable use and misuse. This can relate to such things as intended use and product labeling, consumer assembly required, product operation, packaging and product removal from packaging, claim substantiation, different use environments, expected product life, and alternative consumer uses.

Intended Use and Product Labeling

When evaluating any consumer product for intended use, several factors must be considered: the manufacturer's stated intent; the product's advertising, promotion, and marketing; and the commonly recognized use of the product.

The manufacturer's stated intent can be in the form of a label on the product or on the packaging. The stated intent is only one factor, and it must be a reasonable one that is consistent with the other factors. For example, if the manufacturer labels a product as suitable for adults and children ages 12 years and up, this may be a reasonable label if it does not conflict with the other factors that determine intended use.

The product's advertising, promotion, and marketing can communicate a clear and specific message about appropriate and reasonable use. The actions and depictions of advertising, promotion, and marketing materials speak loudly and can be used to define reasonable and appropriate use even if they conflict with product labeling. For example, if the packaging label states that the product is for ages eight years and up but the advertising shows three-year-olds using it, then it can be construed that the product is appropriate for use by three-year-olds.

The product's commonly recognized use is also an important consideration. For example, a plush teddy bear is commonly recognized as appropriate for a one- or two-year-old. Therefore, a plush teddy bear provided as a separate premium with the purchase of an adult pair of shoes would still logically be considered appropriate for a one-year-old. The teddy bear would be required to meet the infant toy safety standards. If it failed to satisfy these standards, it would be considered a banned hazardous product, notwithstanding the fact that it was sold as part of an adult product.

Consumer Assembly

The consumer-friendly approach, naturally, is to eliminate or minimize consumer assembly. Any assembly that is required must be simple and obvious, easy (requiring a low level of force and coordination), foolproof such that misassembly is either impossible or easily corrected, and reasonably safe to perform.

If general tools are required, this information should be conspicuously stated on the package. If special tools are required, they should be provided with the product.

Product Operation

Proper operation of the product by the consumer must be intuitive and foolproof. For example, turning knobs in a clockwise direction should increase intensity, and turning counterclockwise should decrease intensity. Any accidental misoperation must not permanently damage the product, render it nonfunctional, or present any unreasonable safety risks.

The assembly and operation of the product should be so easy and obvious that instructions are not even required, or are at least greatly simplified.

Product Packaging

Packaging should be minimized, as it is expensive and ultimately wasteful. Use only enough to protect the product from damage during shipment, handling, and storage and to provide necessary communication about the product to the consumer. Packaging may also be required to prevent the pilfering of separate component parts. The packaging must also be convenient and safe for the consumer to remove. It should be designed such that any tools required for opening should be limited to those that can be used safely, for example, a screwdriver or a scissors; knives or razor blades should not be required to open it or remove the product.

Claim Substantiation

A claim is any representation, whether stated or implied, concerning a product or service attribute. This includes representations of appearance, size, weight, content, operation, use, and performance.

For example, if a declaration of net weight appears on the product's package, it must be verified and documented that the production process is delivering product that conforms to the net weight claim. At a minimum, this means verifying that the mean minus one standard deviation of the process output is equal to or greater than the declared weight. This equates to approximately 84% of the process population meeting or exceeding the declared weight. Sometimes two or even three standard deviations might be desired and specified, depending on the type of claim and its importance to the consumer.

It is very important that all product and service representations to the consumer be accurate and substantiated with testing data and information. Consumer delight results when the organization exceeds expectations and delivers more than was promised. Never exaggerate or fail to substantiate any claim directed to the consumer.

And finally, avoid using general terms such as "safe" or "reliable" in product claims. The consumer (and the consumer's attorney) could interpret this type of absolute claim to mean that the product can withstand *all* misuse, not just reasonably foreseeable misuse. Instead, use terms such as "safety tested" or "reliability tested"—claims that can be readily substantiated.

Different Use Environments

It should be recognized that the product will be used in various environments. The product may see environments of extreme temperatures, varying levels of humidity, rain, fog, sunshine and ultraviolet radiation, salt water, dust, and even ozone. The product concept evaluation must consider that the product will be used in various environmental conditions. The product design must ensure that the product will withstand reasonably foreseeable environments of consumer use.

Expected Product Life

Product reliability is a critical component of product safety. It is vital that the product be designed, manufactured, tested, and verified against life requirements that exceed the expectations of the consumer. Since there can be significant consumer variation in expected product life, a conservative approach with a factor of safety in the life requirement is necessary. A product safety rule of thumb is to test and qualify products for three times the normal lifetime of the product. During the product concept evaluation, the foreseeable use assessment must include a consideration for product reliability.

Alternative Consumer Uses

An awareness of alternative uses is especially important when establishing requirements for children's products. The concept evaluation should include an assessment of reasonably foreseeable ways the product might be used that go beyond the intended use. For example, a large inflatable ball might be used (misused) by the consumer as a safety flotation device in a swimming pool or at the beach. This must be considered in the way the product is designed and labeled.

Another example is childproof caps for adult medicine containers. Even though the container is clearly intended for adults, some children will try to use the product in imitation of the parent. For this reason, the container caps are made to be childproof.

Figure 3.2 shows a picture of what seems to be a preschool toy bus with little figures that can be placed in the seats on the

Figure 3.2   A preschool toy bus or a roller skate?

bus. The top part of the bus (roof) is open to facilitate placing the figures in the seats. When you look at this picture, is that what you see?

When some preschoolers look at the bus, they see roller skates! They put their feet into the bus and move around pretending to be roller skating. This is considered to be a reasonably foreseeable alternative use, and the product should be designed to withstand this type of use.

HUMAN FACTORS

Human factors relate to human characteristics, capabilities, and physical properties. When evaluating new product concepts it is especially important to consider the physical (anthropometric) measurements, strengths, and capabilities of the consumer.

In the toy industry it is critical to know the biomechanical forces that a child can exert on a product during use and abuse. This includes tensile forces with the hands and with other children. It includes compression forces with the mouth (biting), hands, and feet. It includes torque abuse with the thumb and forefinger or the thumb and all of the fingers. It includes bending forces (moments) and also impact forces due to throwing, stomping, and kicking.

The University of Michigan Medical Center has performed several child strength and anthropometric studies for the CPSC. Some examples are as follows:

1. *Strength Characteristics of U.S. Children for Product Safety Design* (1975), by Clyde Owings, Don Chaffin, Richard Snyder, and Richard Norcutt

2. *Gripping Strength Measurements of Children for Product Safety Design* (1977), by Clyde Owings, Richard Norcutt, Richard Snyder, D. Henry Golomb, and Kathie Lloyd

3. *Size and Shape of the Head and Neck from Birth to Four Years* (1986), by Lawrence Schneider, Richard Lehman, Melissa Pflug, and Clyde Owings

This kind of human factors information is necessary when performing comprehensive safety assessments during new product concept evaluations.

One of the major concerns with children's products is airway obstruction resulting from small parts. This can include choking on a small part that is lodged in the throat (oral cavity or oropharynx) or aspiration of a small part into the bronchi or lungs. Human factors information shows that certain shapes are much more likely to create an airway obstruction because they can easily seal against the anatomical structures of the airway. These shapes—spheres, cones, teardrops, and egg shapes (see Figure 3.3)—are also more likely to be put into the mouth because they are smooth, rounded, and inviting. The objective is to either avoid those shapes or make them large enough to preclude the possibility of choking or aspiration.

Human factors information also alerts us to shapes that may easily slide down the front part of the throat but be very difficult

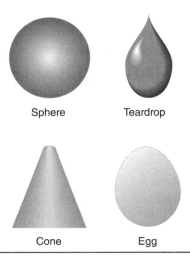

Sphere   Teardrop

Cone   Egg

Figure 3.3 Hazardous small shapes for young children.

to remove. Figure 3.4 shows some objects that contain projections that may become lodged in the soft tissues of the oral cavity or throat. These shapes create a "fishhook" effect, which means they easily move in one direction (down the throat) but not in the opposite direction (removal from the throat). These shapes would need to be changed or made larger to preclude their fitting into a child's mouth.

Figure 3.5 shows two small girl figurines, one with pigtails and one without. The figurine with the pigtails is the early design version, which presented the fishhook effect. The

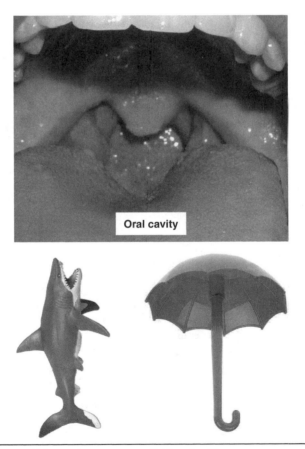

Figure 3.4   Objects that create a fishhook effect.

Old—with pigtails   **New—without pigtails**

Figure 3.5   An early design version showing a fishhook effect and the corrected version.

figurine with the haircut (no pigtails) is the corrected version. Human factors information helps us ensure that new product concepts have designed-in safety.

TECHNICAL COLLABORATION INPUT

During the concept evaluation stage of product development, the knowledge acquired through technical collaboration is applied to the hazard identification checklists, the foreseeable use and misuse evaluation, and the human factors assessments. The application of this knowledge serves to ensure that the product concept evaluation is thorough and circumspect.

When evaluating entirely new product concepts with which an organization has little technical experience, there is a real danger in proceeding ahead with blissful ignorance. Winston Churchill stated that true genius resides in the capacity for evaluation of uncertain, hazardous, and conflicting information. Although this statement may be true, don't count on "true genius" from your organization. You don't need true genius, and you don't need to take chances with hazards, conflicts, and uncertainty. You just need to use the experience and expertise of your technical resources network to allow evaluations to be conducted with accurate and complete information. This is excellence.

WARNING LABEL PROBLEMS

Avoiding Hazard Elimination

The first problem associated with warnings is that they are sometimes used in lieu of addressing the actual product hazard. It can be a lot easier to simply add a warning label than to actually change the product design to eliminate the hazard. Our legal system generally presumes that users will read and heed adequate warnings. A product is generally considered to be nondefective if it contains an adequate warning and is safe for use if the warning is followed. This can be a real incentive for manufacturers to add plenty of warnings to ensure against future product liability. The eagerness to rely on warnings can lead to some pretty silly product labels that contain unnecessary information. Added warnings can dilute the conspicuousness and significance of the warning that is truly important. They can also lead to consumer complacency whereby the consumer ignores all of the warnings. Figure 3.6 shows some real examples of ill-advised product warnings.

Failing to Influence User Behavior

The second problem associated with warnings is that they are often ineffective. In order for a warning label to be effective, it must trigger five consumer responses:

1. It must be noticed. Does it attract the consumer's attention?

2. It must be read. Is the consumer likely to read it?

3. It must be understood. Does the consumer comprehend it?

4. It must be remembered. Will the consumer recall it?

5. It must be complied with. Will it influence consumer behavior?

Warning label effectiveness, therefore, depends on several conditions all happening: (1) The consumer must be able to read, (2) the consumer must be alert, sober, and not overloaded with other information, (3) the label must be in a convenient and

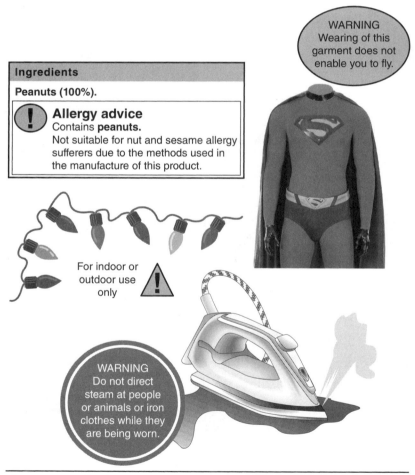

Figure 3.6 Ill-advised product warnings.

noticeable location and be large enough with sufficient contrast to be conspicuous, (4) the label must be brief, legible, and easily understood, (5) the label must make the consumer believe that there is a significant hazard, and (6) the consumer must not accept the risk or consider the cost of compliance to be greater than the cost of ignoring the label. The probability of all these conditions being satisfied is not very high, and that is why warnings often fail to work.

Inappropriate for Children

In the toy industry, warnings are generally not an option, because it is reasonably foreseeable that young children cannot or will not read and heed them. The product must not present unreasonable risks of injury during any reasonably foreseeable use and misuse. Warnings, therefore, are not an option for most children's products. The only exception would be warnings intended for the parent or caregiver, usually for assistance with purchasing decisions, adult assembly, or adult supervision.

Summary

The primary objective is always to make products inherently safe so that warnings are not needed. Some products, however, may include an inherent hazard, such as swimming pools or appliances that require electricity. When a hazard cannot be eliminated from the product design, the objective is to provide a guard or some other means of reducing the danger to an acceptable level. Warnings should always be a last resort.

CONCEPT RISK ASSESSMENT

The risk assessment of a concept is defined as the risk analysis and the risk evaluation of that concept. *Risk analysis* is the identification of hazards and the estimation of associated risks. *Risk evaluation* is the judgment of risk acceptability. Therefore, the concept of *risk assessment* is the identification of all potential hazards, the estimation of the associated hazard risks, and the judgment of whether the risks that cannot be reasonably eliminated are acceptable.

After the potential hazards have been identified, foreseeable use and misuse have been assessed, human factors have been considered, and technical collaboration has occurred, the risks can be assessed and the concept can be evaluated. The concept evaluation would include answering the following questions:

1. Is this a reasonably safe product for the user?

2. What can the user do with the product that would be considered reasonably foreseeable misuse?

3. What extreme environments might the product see?

4. What standards and regulations must be satisfied?

5. Will this product be state of the art in the industry?

6. Are there warnings or instructions that should be considered?

Two other analytical tools can be helpful when evaluating new product concepts: failure modes and effects analysis and fault tree analysis.

Failure Modes and Effects Analysis

Failure modes and effects analysis (FMEA) is a tool for determining the effects a component failure would have on the entire product. For each identified failure mode of each component, the consequences to the product are assessed. The data provide the bases for determining how and where component changes can best be made to improve the probability that the product will function successfully. Because FMEA begins at the component part level and determines the effects at the product level, it is sometimes called a "bottom-up" methodology.

The main purpose of FMEA, then, is to evaluate the frequency and consequences of critical component failures. Since a product can be made up of many components, it is often prohibitive to evaluate all potential component failures. Engineering judgment is usually used to identify the critical components. These critical components are then systematically examined.

Fault Tree Analysis

Fault tree analysis (FTA) is the reverse of FMEA in that it starts by supposing that the product has failed (resulting in an accident) and then considers the possible causes that could have led to the failure. Conditions, events, and component failures are considered to find the whole set of critical paths that lead to the product failure (accident). The most critical and probable sequence of events that could produce the product failure is determined, and ways to avoid these origins and causes are identified. Because FTA begins at the product or top level, it is sometimes called a "top-down" methodology.

4

Design Qualification
Confirming Safety, Reliability, and Manufacturability

When you design it, think how you would feel if you had to fly it! Safety first!

—DONALD WILLS DOUGLAS

*D*esign qualification is the process of confirming that the product design satisfies all safety, reliability, and manufacturability requirements. This chapter reviews the major activities that must occur to achieve a qualified design.

DESIGN REVIEW

A *design review* is a product development milestone in which a design is formally evaluated by a multidisciplined product development team to ensure that all concerns are resolved and all requirements are incorporated, and to guide it toward achieving safety, reliability, manufacturability, costing, and schedule specifications. The design review is a critique of the entire product design that includes the following:

1. Materials and component parts

2. Product packaging

3. Planned instructions and labels

4. Engineering drawings

5. Product definition and specifications, including performance claims

6. Manufacturing process plans and specifications

7. Looks-like, works-like prototype review

The design review process begins after the concept evaluation has been completed, approved, and turned over to the product development team. The product development team needs to include a representative from the following disciplines:

1. Product engineering/Costing

2. Design

3. Manufacturing/Process engineering/Sourcing

4. Marketing/Sales

5. Quality/Reliability/Safety engineering

As the product proceeds through the product development process, a series of design review team meetings occurs until the entire product design critique has been satisfactorily completed. This is when the product design and the manufacturing process are well defined, and the safety, reliability, cost and schedule objectives are deemed feasible. It is at this point that design qualification occurs.

In summary, design qualification ensures that the designed product, if manufactured, will satisfy all of the design specifications and requirements. Further, if concept evaluation and design qualification are done correctly, it will save a lot of time and cost for later stages of development and manufacturing and beyond to consumer success.

SAFETY CHECKLIST

The safety checklist is an important tool for ensuring that new product designs are evaluated thoroughly and accurately for safety risks. It serves to stimulate thought and guide brainstorming to ensure that design risks and safety considerations are addressed in the product design. It even provides a means for documenting design decisions for safety.

An example of a safety checklist that might be used in the toy industry is shown in Figure 4.1. It is important to note that the safety checklist is a living, evolving tool. It should be continually updated with knowledge of past proven design experiences, information from the technical collaboration network, and education from exposure to industry issues concerning emerging hazards.

It is important that every question contained in the safety checklist be reviewed prior to and during the design review process. The detailed review may take one or two hours to complete, but it will help ensure that no important considerations are overlooked.

Occasionally there may be situations where the product concept being considered is very well defined at the concept evaluation stage of development. In these situations it may be appropriate to use the safety checklist tool during the concept evaluation. It is desirable to use the safety checklist at the earliest stage of development, but often this is at design qualification, where the product is reasonably defined.

Labeling
Functional sharp points that require cautionary statement?
Adult assembly statement required where child hazards exist?
Hot surfaces statements?
Food additives that require allergy statements?
Art materials that require LHAMA labeling?
Batteries requiring battery statements?
Assembly required and tools required statements?
Transmitters requiring FCC registration?

Materials
Vinyl-styrene contact and plasticizer migration issues?
Food/Ingestibles—FDA ingredients, GRAS (generally recognized as safe) list?
Food-contact plastics—FDA recognized?
Metals—oxidation/rust/heavy elements prevention?
Toxicity and allergenicity—inhalation, dermal, oral?
Preservative efficacy—foods, liquids, nutrients?
Fungicides—water reservoirs, food-contact materials?

Function
Obvious/Easy—assembly issues or incorrect assembly issues?
Stability issues—tip over, non-skid?
Suffocation—vent holes, cup-shape objects, pillow-like objects?
Strangulation—cords, straps, and safety breakaway feature?
Entrapment—finger, hand, foot, head, and hair?
Pinch points—hinges, folding mechanisms, spring clearances?
Visual obstruction—masks, helmets, peripheral vision?
Sounds/Noise levels—impulsive and continuous?
Light intensity—ophthalmologist evaluation?
Metal detection—sewn products, stuffed toys, modeling clay?
Batteries—inaccessible, circuit protection, low-battery indicator?
Projectiles—energy level, resilient tip, not small size?
Overheating, shock, and burn potential?
Projection hazards—axles, conical shapes, bath toy impalement?
Impaction hazards—to the ears, mouth/throat, or genitals?

Asphyxiation
Hazardous shapes avoided—sphere, cone, teardrop, egg?
Fishhook effect—unidirectional object that could lodge in throat?
Redundancy—small parts reliably secured?
Small parts avoided—mouth objects, magnets, preschool objects?

Consumer use/misuse
Packaging issues—difficult for consumer to open?
Product/Package shelf-life issues?
Storage issues—how will consumer store it?
Repair issues—how will consumer try to repair it?
Disposal issues—how will consumer dispose of it?
Compatibility issues—is it compatible with other products?
Use environments—salt, soapy, pure water; sand; UV; vibration?
Foreseeable misuse by nonintended users?

Figure 4.1 Example of a toy safety checklist for design review.

RELIABILITY

Investing a lot of time, cost, and effort to make sure that the consumer receives a safe product is essential, but it is not sufficient. The manufacturer must also make sure that the product will remain safe during the reasonable life of the product. This is why reliability is such an important part of product safety. A safe product must be a reliable product.

Reliability is defined as the probability that a product will perform its specified function satisfactorily for a specified period of time under specified operating conditions. The terms "specified function," "specified period of time," and "specified operating conditions" mean what the consumer reasonably expects, not just what the manufacturer might include in its specifications. The term "satisfactorily" means meeting reasonable consumer expectations and meeting them in a reasonably safe manner.

The subject of reliability, therefore, includes discussions on product safety related to function, life, and environmental conditions. This includes some key tools and guidelines for product reliability performance.

Functional Performance

A product reliability assessment includes evaluations for functional performance. All functional aspects of the product must be tested to ensure that the consumer can easily and safely use the product. This includes any consumer assembly that is required. The assembly and function of the product must be simple and obvious. Additionally, the product must be evaluated for reasonably foreseeable misuse to ensure that functional performance and safety performance are not compromised.

Product Life

It is important that a product be designed, manufactured, tested, and verified to life requirements that exceed the expectations of the consumer. There is, however, no common life test standard, because an appropriate life test requirement is highly dependent on the type of product or component being tested. For example, it may be a high-use product (bicycle) or a low-use product (pull toy), a primary function (electric train engine) or a secondary function (the train whistle), or a one-time-per-use function (on-off switch) or a continuous-use function (electric motor). There are too many variables to establish one general specification. Information to assist in establishing appropriate life test requirements can be obtained from consumer-use history of similar past products, consumer research and surveys, benchmarking with best-in-class companies, and testing competitor products.

Shelf Life

Shelf life evaluation of products that are perishable is another aspect of product reliability assessment. *Shelf life* is the amount of time a perishable item is given before it is considered unsuitable for consumer use. It is the manufacturer's recommended time that the product can be stored without becoming ineffective or defective in quality level.

A high-temperature accelerated aging test can be conducted to determine moisture loss (weight loss) through packaging and to evaluate product function after an extended period of time. Arrhenius law relates chemical reaction rate to temperature level. Basically, the reaction rate doubles for every 10°C increase in temperature. For example, a product stored for one day at a temperature of 50°C (122°F) equates to being stored for eight days at 20°C (68°F). The reaction rate doubles at 30°C, quadruples at 40°C, and is eight times greater at 50°C. To understand how a sealed package might perform for a period of six months, one could subject it to 122°F for about 22 or 23 days before conducting the evaluation.

It should be noted that the Arrhenius model is valid for shelf life testing only when the test temperature is at or below the level where there is no material content breakdown due to excessive heat. For any given product there is a temperature limit above which shelf life testing cannot be performed because the materials will degrade.

Battery Life

Battery life is another reliability consideration. Battery compartment design (i.e., number, size, and type of batteries) and product current draw determine how long the product will function before the batteries need to be replaced. This is always an important concern for ensuring consumer satisfaction. Additionally, a weak-battery condition in a product should either be obvious to the consumer or be indicated to the consumer in some manner. Otherwise, the consumer may think that the product has failed and may return it or even try to repair it.

Environmental Conditions

A product may reasonably be subjected to various and extreme environmental conditions during transportation and also during use by the consumer. The environmental testing begins with transportation testing (vibration and impact) of the packaged product. If the product will be air shipped, it may need to be vacuum tested if product leakage is a concern. In addition to standard high temperatures (140°F) and low temperatures (0°F), the product may need to be evaluated for high ultraviolet (UV) and ozone exposure if it will be used outside. Some products may need to be tested to ensure that they are machine washable and dishwasher safe. The testing environments will need to simulate the reasonably foreseeable consumer use and misuse.

Multiple Environment Over-Stress Test

Multiple environment over-stress test (MEOST) is an accelerated life test method with thermal and vibration cycling intended to quickly identify and resolve design weaknesses.

The objective is not to determine product reliability but rather to fail the product in order to determine the weak links. MEOST weeds out any marginal designs and improves the reliability of the product. It also substantially increases the probability of success at the product qualification stage of development. Keki Bhote's outstanding book, *World Class Reliability* (American Management Association, 2004), provides an excellent presentation on MEOST.

Redundancy

In reliability and safety, *redundancy* is the duplication of critical components to increase the overall reliability of the product. An example is a brake light with two lightbulbs. If one component (lightbulb) fails, the second component still provides service so that the product (brake light) does not fail. Redundancy is a way to ensure very high levels of product reliability when using components that offer only moderate reliability levels.

Figure 4.2 shows how a component with 99% reliability (1% failure rate) can be used redundantly to achieve 99.99% reliability (0.01% failure rate).

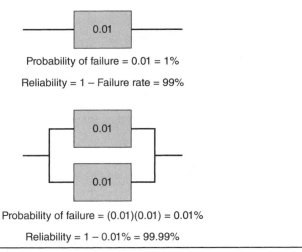

Probability of failure = 0.01 = 1%

Reliability = 1 − Failure rate = 99%

Probability of failure = (0.01)(0.01) = 0.01%

Reliability = 1 − 0.01% = 99.99%

Figure 4.2   Redundancy improves reliability.

Fail-Safe Design

A *fail-safe design* is one that ensures that no unsafe consequences occur if and when the product fails. In other words, the product remains safe if it fails. Some examples of fail-safe designs are as follows:

1. An elevator with a governor safety mechanism that makes contact with the guide rail to decelerate the car in the event that the elevator begins to accelerate too quickly as a result of cable failure

2. A traffic signal that automatically defaults to a flashing all-red rather than displaying a dangerous all-green in all directions

3. An electrically operated consumer product that contains a fuse that causes the product to fail if temperatures become excessive

It is important to consider the significance of all potential functional failures to ensure that no unsafe effects occur from any failure or combination of failures.

PROCESS CAPABILITY ANALYSIS

Product reliability and safety are highly dependent on manufacturing process capability. If the process is not capable of delivering product that meets the requirements necessary for reliability and safety, the design is not qualified. A capable process must meet three criteria:

1. *The process is completely defined and documented.*

2. *The process is centered.* This means that the calculated average of the process output is equal to the specification requirement.

3. *The process has acceptable variation.* This means that the width of the process is reasonably less than the width of the specification. The *process width* is the difference between the upper process limit (UPL) and the lower process limit (LPL), which is defined as six standard deviations of process variation. The *specification width* is the difference between the upper specification tolerance limit (USL) and the lower specification tolerance limit (LSL).

Documented Process

The first step in ensuring process capability is to completely define the process. All relevant processing conditions must be documented, including specific materials used; exact equipment used; precise equipment settings (and equipment calibration verification); all processing sequence steps, including processing parameters such as times, temperatures, and pressures; all operator procedures and methods used; and a processing facility description including ambient conditions.

The process documentation must describe essentially everything about the process inputs and processing activities that produce the output that is tested and evaluated. In fact, without the process first being fully defined and documented, the testing and evaluation of the output should not occur. Process capability has not occurred if the process has not been completely defined and documented.

Centered Process

When the average output of a process (running without any assignable causes of variation) is exactly the same as the specification, the process is said to be *centered*. Figure 4.3 depicts a centered process.

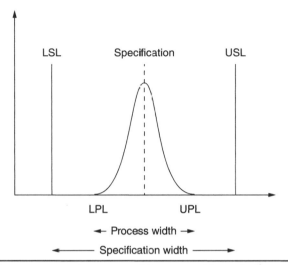

Figure 4.3   A centered process with acceptable variation.

Acceptable Variation

Process capability (Cp) is defined as specification width divided by process width. When the specification width is twice the process width, the Cp is 2.0. A corrected process capability factor (Cpk) is used when the process is not centered on the specification. Since we are considering only centered processes, the Cpk will equal the Cp. Referring again to Figure 4.3, we can see that the process shown is approximately one-half the specification width, resulting in a Cpk of approximately 2.0.

For critical reliability and product safety specifications, a minimum Cpk of 2.0 is recommended, which equates to a theoretical defective rate of a few defective parts per billion parts produced. This represents a capable process that will deliver acceptable performance, especially when used with other tools discussed later in this book, such as safety factors and process control.

SAFETY SPECIFICATION DEVELOPMENT

A *product safety specification* is a written document that describes in detail all of the testing and evaluation requirements a specific product must satisfy to be considered safety-qualified for consumer use. The product safety specification is used by the testing laboratory to ensure that all required tests and evaluations are performed correctly and that test reports properly document product compliance with safety requirements. It is also used to ensure that suppliers and purchasers of the product understand and agree to all product safety requirements. It may be referenced in a manufacturing agreement or a licensing agreement.

The product safety specification is completely developed and approved by the end of design qualification, because a qualified design must incorporate all safety concerns and requirements. The specification, therefore, is immediately available for the testing and qualification of the product prior to production start. The development of a product safety specification may include information from many different sources, as is shown in Figure 4.4.

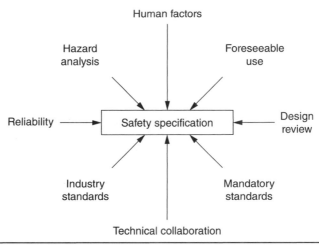

Figure 4.4   Product safety specification input information.

CLAIM SUBSTANTIATION

One consideration of product liability and product integrity is the accurate representation of the product to the consumer. It is therefore very important to ensure that all product claims directed to the consumer be accurate and substantiated with testing data and information.

A claim is any representation, whether stated or implied, concerning any product or service attribute. This includes representations of appearance, size, weight, content, operation, use, and performance. All claims should be incorporated into the product specification, and they should be tested and approved during product qualification.

Consumer delight results when the organization exceeds expectations and delivers more than was promised. Never exaggerate or fail to substantiate any claim directed to the consumer.

SUMMARY

Design qualification is the third of the seven elements of product safety excellence, and both the technical collaboration and the concept evaluation elements feed directly into design qualification. These three elements (of the seven total elements) focus exclusively on product design, which highlights the importance of design in achieving product safety excellence.

The vast majority of quality failures, product recalls, and product liability lawsuits are a direct result of poor design. The emphasis must be on getting the design right. As Mr. Douglas stated, when you design it, think how you would feel if you had to fly it.

5

Supplier Qualification

Verifying Capabilities, Capacities, Controls, and Commitment

Trust, but verify.

—RONALD REAGAN

*S*upplier qualification is the process of verifying that a potential new supplier is capable of and committed to satisfying all requirements, and that its manufacturing process capabilities, capacities, and controls are acceptable before it is approved. This chapter reviews the major activities that must occur to qualify a supplier. It is important that all product suppliers be evaluated and qualified.

QUALITY SYSTEMS AUDIT

The systems and processes that produce the product primarily determine the success or failure of production. If the quality systems and processes are right, then the safety, reliability, and quality of the design-qualified product will be right as well. Further, since a supplier is essentially an extension of the manufacturer's organization, it is important that the supplier's quality systems be complete, reliable, and acceptable to the manufacturer. The quality systems audit is used by the manufacturer to qualify the supplier from a product safety and quality standpoint.

The quality systems audit usually includes a checklist to ensure that the audit is thorough and complete. Some checklists are very detailed and many pages long, but no matter how long or brief they are, the primary objective is to assess the supplier's probability of delivering product that consistently satisfies all safety, reliability, quality, cost, and schedule requirements. A top 10 list of questions for evaluating a potential supplier's capability is shown in Figure 5.1.

---

1. Is top management committed to completely understanding and satisfying all of your requirements?

2. Does the supplier have adequate capability and capacity to satisfy production quantities, schedules, and product specifications?

3. Are process capability evaluations documented with adequate process capability (Cpk) values?

4. Are "real time" process control systems used to allow appropriate process adjustments to prevent the manufacture of nonconforming product?

5. Is there an established and practiced procedure for the evaluation, implementation, and control of product and process changes?

6. Are root causes determined and prevention-based corrective action initiated when an unsatisfactory trend is indicated?

7. Is there a system for use, calibration, and preventive maintenance of test and production equipment?

8. Is "good housekeeping" maintained, and are clean, orderly, and secure storage facilities used to safeguard materials and product?

9. Are manufacturing processes well engineered, balanced, and lean to minimize work-in-process inventory, handling, and other non-value-added activities?

10. Is there a documented and practiced system for the selection and qualification of material suppliers and subcontractors?

Figure 5.1   Top 10 questions for assessing supplier capability.

A potential supplier that has a good record of reliable performance may not need to have an on-site visit for the audit. There are times when a self-audit against the manufacturer's audit criteria may be sufficient, especially for relatively non-critical products. In other cases, it will be necessary for the audit to be performed on-site by the manufacturer before supplier qualification can occur.

At a minimum the quality systems audit must ensure that four criteria are satisfied:

1. The supplier's management understands and is committed to achieving the manufacturer's requirements

2. The supplier has the process capability and capacity to meet all requirements

3. The supplier understands and has signed the manufacturing agreement

4. The supplier understands and is committed to the manufacturer's change control requirements

Each of the four criteria will be covered separately in more detail.

MANAGEMENT COMMITMENT

The most important predictor of supplier success is the attitude and behavior of the supplier's top management. The president, the business owner, and senior executive management must be absolutely committed to product safety and understanding and satisfying all of your requirements. They must inspire this commitment in their managers, supervisors, and employees down the line and demonstrate it in their communications and actions throughout the organization.

When the supplier's management is truly committed to completely understanding and completely satisfying all of your requirements, the probability of success is high. Conversely, if they don't show a lot of interest or are reluctant to accept your requirements, the probability of success is low.

SUPPLIER CAPABILITIES AND CAPACITIES

The evaluation of a potential supplier must consider supplier manufacturing capabilities and capacities. The manufacturing equipment and tooling must be commensurate with the product and production requirements. This means that the quantity, type, precision, and accuracy of the equipment and tooling must be consistent with your standards, requirements, and expectations for the following:

1. Product safety and reliability tolerances—capability

2. Product quality and consistency—capability

3. Production output and demand—capacity

4. Product lead times and schedules—capacity

It is important to note that both manufacturing capability and manufacturing capacity are necessary for success. If capacity issues are not realized up front, big problems can occur at the back end. A typical supplier will try very hard to solve a capacity problem and may employ one or more of the following:

1. The supplier will undoubtedly try to increase capacity of the process, probably beyond the capability limits of the approved equipment

2. The supplier may try to add substitute equipment that is inferior to the qualified equipment

3. The supplier may try to subcontract additional product, probably from a source unknown to you, with unknown reliability

If the capacity problem is big enough, the supplier may try all three of these deviations in an earnest attempt to fix the problem. Unfortunately, each of these deviations is a recipe for potential major product safety problems such as the following:

1. Safety standards violations and fines

2. Consumer complaints and injury

3. Defective returns

4. Product recall

5. Product liability lawsuits

All of this must be prevented by including the manufacturing capacity assessment with the manufacturing capability assessment when qualifying suppliers. Change control is also a mandatory supplier requirement and will be covered later in this chapter.

MANUFACTURING AGREEMENT

A manufacturing agreement typically involves a customer using a supplier to manufacture products that the customer will sell in the marketplace. The purpose of the manufacturing agreement is to ensure that there is a clear and documented understanding of the supplier's responsibilities and obligations to the customer, including remedies, penalties, and customer protections for any breach by the supplier. The customer protections include product recall and product liability indemnification and also a requirement for appropriate supplier product liability insurance.

A product safety manager will want to include certain basic requirements in a manufacturing agreement. Figure 5.2 lists 10 of the most important. The term "COMPANY" is used to indicate where the customer's name (your company) would

1. COMPANY has the right to inspect and test products and reject any nonconformances.
2. COMPANY has the right to enter and inspect manufacturing and storage facilities.
3. Manufacturer complies with all applicable laws, rules, regulations, and COMPANY policies and standards.
4. Manufacturer indemnifies COMPANY against any and all lawsuits, losses, injuries, and expenses resulting from breach of agreement.
5. Manufacturer agrees to repair, replace, or correct any defective or nonconforming product.
6. COMPANY may return nonconforming product to manufacturer at its risk and expense.
7. Manufacturer shall destroy, pursuant to COMPANY instructions, all substandard products not purchased by COMPANY and shall provide to COMPANY a written certification of destruction.
8. COMPANY has no obligation to purchase substandard products.
9. Manufacturer shall use trademarks only on products purchased by COMPANY and only in a manner approved by COMPANY.
10. Once product has been qualified by COMPANY, manufacturer shall make no changes in design, processing, materials, or manufacturing facility, nor depart in any fashion from the specifications, quality standards, or appearance of any product without first obtaining written approval from COMPANY.

Figure 5.2 Checklist for manufacturing agreement.

appear, and the term "Manufacturer" is used to indicate the supplier name.

CHANGE CONTROL

A substantial amount of time, effort, and expense is required to ensure a comprehensive product design, to thoroughly test and qualify a product for production, and to thoroughly substantiate and document a product's safety and reliability. When this occurs, there is great satisfaction in knowing that safe and reliable product is being delivered to your customer and sold to and enjoyed by your consumer. The confidence in knowing that your documentation is complete and sound allows for restful nights and blissful days.

Then what happens? You suddenly find out that last month your supplier ran out of the approved material and, on its own, substituted a different, unknown material. You are unaware of the material composition and what, if any, testing was performed. The supplier is unaware of all of the safety and reliability considerations that resulted in the original material selection, so it couldn't possibly know if the substitute material is feasible.

Now, suddenly, all of that comprehensive and sound documentation has nothing to do with the product you have been shipping to your customers and consumers. What happens if you are contacted by the CPSC and it wants to review your documentation because it has just received a serious consumer injury notice? Maybe you have a good manufacturing agreement and your supplier will indemnify you against product recall and liability expenses, but do you really want to face the damage that this will do to your company name and brand and to consumer trust and loyalty?

Unauthorized changes must be prevented. This must be an important discussion with the supplier's management before the supplier is qualified. The top management of the supplier must completely understand, fully embrace, and strongly communicate throughout the entire organization a "no unauthorized changes" policy. This means that once you have qualified the product for production, the supplier will make none of the following changes without first obtaining your written approval:

1. Product design

2. Processing

3. Materials used in production

4. Manufacturing facility or location

It is recognized that change is good. Improvements are made through change. Having a policy is not meant to discourage

---

Continuing Product Guaranty

We hereby agree and guarantee that once COMPANY approves the supplied product for production/shipping, **no change in design, processing, manufacturing location, or materials used in production of the product will occur without our obtaining prior written approval from COMPANY.**

We agree to indemnify and hold COMPANY harmless from and against any and all costs, expenses, losses, liability, and damages suffered as a result of the breach of any term or provision of this agreement by us, our agents, or our representatives.

This guaranty is a continuing guaranty that applies to all products and shipments shipped to or on behalf of COMPANY by this company or any of its subsidiaries or associated companies.

| Company name | Authorized signature (company officer) | Title of person signing |

| Address | Name of person signing | Date |

Figure 5.3   Example of a "no unauthorized changes" guaranty.

change. It is meant to eliminate and forever ban any and all *unauthorized* changes.

The "no unauthorized changes" policy must be a prominent part of your manufacturing agreements. Further, it is so important that it should be a separate guaranty that is signed by the supplier's CEO or designated officer. Figure 5.3 shows an example of such a guaranty. Note that the term "COMPANY" is used where your company name would normally appear.

STRATEGIC PARTNERSHIP

A higher level of relationship and performance with your qualified supplier is a strategic partnership. In a strategic partnership you need to provide your partner supplier with frequent visits, training, coaching, larger and growing volumes, much reduced competition, and higher profits and return on investment. In return, you should expect from your partner supplier a commitment to reduce and eventually terminate all work with your competition, help with the next tier of suppliers (nonpartners), and a willingness to network with your other partner suppliers.

It is important to recognize that not all of your suppliers should be strategic partners. In order to guarantee a stable and growing order flow to your strategic partners, you need a base of next-tier suppliers that have a flexible (nonstable) order flow in order to accommodate your strategic partners during times of variable sales orders. By varying and reducing order allocations to these next-tier suppliers, you can maintain a stable order flow to your strategic partners.

Critical products requiring special processing equipment and procedures or products in which manufacturing precision is desired are especially good candidates for strategic partner suppliers. Any products requiring extra manufacturing attention because of special product safety standards and requirements are also good candidates.

6

Product Qualification

Documenting Design and Process and Testing Conformance

One test result is worth one thousand expert opinions.

—WERNHER VON BRAUN

Product qualification is the process of determining product acceptability for production. The product qualification process includes the following steps:

1. Documenting the production process

2. Manufacturing production-representative sample product

3. Testing the sample product against all product safety, reliability, and quality specifications and requirements

4. Achieving acceptable test results

5. Documenting all test results

When all of these steps have been completed, the product is said to be qualified and is ready for the production start milestone. The term "production pilot" is often used to define the product development milestone when product qualification occurs. Often there are earlier "engineering pilot" milestones that serve to debug various aspects of the product and the process prior to attempting the production pilot and full product qualification.

PRODUCTION PROCESS DOCUMENTATION

It is imperative that the actual production process be completely defined and documented in the same manner as described for process capability analysis in Chapter 4. All relevant processing conditions must be documented, including specific materials used; exact equipment used; precise equipment settings (and equipment calibration verification); all processing sequence steps and processing parameters such as times, temperatures, pressures, and so forth; all operator procedures and methods used; and a processing facility description including ambient conditions.

The process documentation must describe essentially everything about the process inputs and processing activities that produce the output that is tested and evaluated. In fact, without the process first being fully defined and documented, the testing and evaluation of the output should not occur. Product qualification does not occur if the process has not been completely defined and documented.

The process documentation from a well-defined, capable process becomes a valuable benchmark tool for future use. If the process output ever changes for no apparent reason, the process qualification documentation will likely provide key information and insight for quick diagnosis and corrective action. Without this information, corrective action could be very time-consuming and costly.

PRODUCTION-REPRESENTATIVE SAMPLES FOR TEST

It is imperative that the samples for test come from the process that was defined and documented and that will be used for actual production. This is so important that some companies have both the factory manufacturing engineer and the quality engineer physically sign each of the master cartons of the product to be tested. Their signatures confirm that the product was manufactured under the identical manufacturing conditions that were documented and established for actual production. The test laboratory does not begin testing unless the product packaging is signed off and the manufacturing processing documentation is submitted.

If the product samples for test were not production-representative, then the test results would not be representative of production product, either. The test results would only serve to substantiate the safety and reliability of some other product that would not actually be produced or sold to your consumer. In this situation, there would be no test documentation for the actual product produced and sold. This would clearly be a serious accident just waiting to happen! Always make sure that samples for product qualification testing come from a well-defined and documented process that will actually be used for production.

Product qualification is used for all new products as well as continuing products with proposed changes that need to be approved. It may also be used for products that have been out of production for an extended time, say three months. The bottom line is that there should always be valid product qualification documentation for every product in production.

TESTING TO FAILURE

It is surprising just how often companies test to only the specification value when they are evaluating whether conformance to the specification has been achieved. For example, if the specification requires the product to withstand a minimum 15-pound tension test, a typical company will apply only 15 pounds to see if the product conforms to the specification. *Testing to specification* means that the test procedure stops when the specification value is achieved (assuming that the product doesn't fail first). With testing to specification, the result is recorded as either a pass or a fail. With pass/fail testing, the results can be very deceiving. This is especially true when the sample sizes for testing are relatively small, such as only 10 samples, 5 samples, or sometimes only 1 sample for a given test.

Consider an example where one sample is taken from a process that is producing defective product at the rate of 50%. This means that the process is producing one defective product for every good product it produces. Now, everyone will agree that a process that is generating 50% defective product is grossly defective and totally unacceptable. Yet, when only one sample is tested to the specification, there is a 50% chance that it will pass!

Now consider an example of a toy product process with an unknown defective rate from which 10 samples are selected and subjected to a 15-pound safety tension test. All 10 samples pass the 15-pound test requirement. Has safety compliance been adequately demonstrated? The answer is no. Using statistics, we can state with 90% confidence that the toy product is less than approximately 20% defective (see Figure 6.1). This means that we can expect (with 90% confidence) fewer than 200,000 defective toys out of every one million produced. This is over 100,000 times higher than what is desired. Observing zero defects with small sample sizes when testing to specification can be very deceiving.

Finally, consider the very extreme example where 1000 product samples are tested to the specification and all of them pass. Figure 6.1 shows that we are now 90% confident that the

Population % defective—Upper limit estimate		
Sample size	90% confidence	95% confidence
5	35%	40%
10	20%	24%
15	14%	17%
20	10%	13%
30	7%	9%
50	4.4%	5.7%
100	2.3%	2.9%
250	0.9%	1.2%
1000	0.23%	0.30%

Figure 6.1 Population percent defective when sample percent defective is zero.

defective rate is less than 0.23%. This is still too far above zero defects for most product safety compliance objectives.

To fully ensure the safety and compliance of a product requires going beyond just testing to specification. It requires testing to failure. An unacceptable or even marginal product design will readily be determined when testing to failure.

Testing to failure means continuing the test beyond the specification until the product finally fails. The force (or torque or any other specification unit of measure) value at failure is recorded for each tested sample. The average force to failure and the standard deviation are calculated, and we can determine statistically the defective rate down to parts per million defective. The information obtained from testing to failure is variable data, which are far superior to the very limited attribute data of pass/fail testing or testing to specification.

Take the example in which 10 product samples were tested to the 15-pound safety tension test, except this time the test will be continued to failure. If, for example, the average failure occurred at 60 pounds with a standard deviation of 8 pounds, we would be confident that safety tension test compliance was demonstrated. If the average failure occurred at 20 pounds with

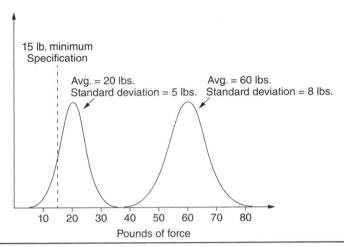

Figure 6.2   Compliance determination using test-to-failure examples.

a standard deviation of 5 pounds, compliance would clearly not be demonstrated (see Figure 6.2).

Only when you test to failure will you know how good or bad your product really is. Product qualification requires testing to failure. Mr. von Braun wisely stated that one test result is worth one thousand expert opinions. I would add that one test to failure is worth one thousand tests to specification.

FACTOR OF SAFETY

It is important to design and manufacture products that are much stronger than is necessary for expected usage and regulatory compliance. This is necessary to allow for variations, imperfections, and degradation that at some level always occur during manufacturing, distribution, and consumer use. The tool to accomplish this is called factor of safety.

Factor of safety is the strength of a product (or component part) above and beyond the expected stress or loads to which the product will be subjected. It is essentially minimum strength divided by maximum stress.

$$\text{Safety factor} = \frac{\text{Minimum strength (of your safety line)}}{\text{Maximum stress (exerted by your weight)}}$$

Figure 6.3   Factor of safety for safety line.

For example, in Figure 6.3, imagine it is you dangling from that cliff and relying on a safety line. Assuming that you weigh 175 pounds and that you might exert a dynamic load of twice your weight during a slip, then the safety line would be rated at a minimum of 350 pounds. If the line is rated at exactly 350 pounds, you have a factor of safety of 1, since minimum strength and maximum stress are equal. However, would you be comfortable in this situation with a safety factor of only 1? You would probably want a safety factor of at least 10—maybe even 20 or more if you have a fear of heights!

Factors of safety, or safety factors, allow for uncertainty in the design and manufacturing process, and they are essentially compensations for imperfection. In situations or conditions that involve varying degrees of uncertainty, you may want to consider safety factors of 3, 5, 10, or even higher. Determining the size of the safety factor should take into consideration other factors that also account for overall product robustness:

1. How serious are the consequences of product failure?

2. What design redundancies exist?

3. How capable are the manufacturing processes; that is, how large are the Cpk values?

4. How well controlled are the manufacturing processes?

Standards Factor of Safety

Another point to consider is that you must have a factor of safety significantly greater than 1.0 applied to your internal standards compared with outside mandatory safety regulations. In other words, your internal standards must always exceed the requirements of any mandatory regulations. There is just too much uncertainty in variations affecting design, material, fabrication, packaging, testing equipment, testing procedure, transportation, and handling to make your internal standards equal to the outside mandatory requirements. It is up to you to choose the safety factor that is appropriate for your product and business, but it should always be greater than 1.0.

TEST DOCUMENTATION

The test reports and other documents from the product qualification process are some of the most important documents in the company. Product qualification test documentation serves several important purposes:

1. Substantiation that the product satisfies safety and reliability requirements

2. Demonstration that the manufacturing process delivers product that satisfies all requirements

3. Documented proof that the product satisfies all mandatory and industry standards

4. Confirmation of a well-defined manufacturing process for reference for future problem solving

5. Validation of testing and conformity requirements in agreements and other legal documents

6. Vital information and support for defense in product liability lawsuits

Because this documentation is so important, it is vital that it be complete and accurate. The test documentation must be complete in that it addresses every requirement in the safety and reliability specifications and in any other product qualification specifications that exist. In other words, there must be no oversights or holes in the documentation that could cause future devastation. The product qualification documentation must show passing results for each and every requirement. Omitting a test result for a product safety requirement is an error that can be particularly devastating when one is later trying to defend the product in a court of law or in a meeting with a regulatory agency.

Once it is verified that the product qualification documentation is complete and accurate, the product is then qualified for production start. These important records must be kept in a secure file for future use. Each company must decide on its own record retention policy, but I would submit that these records should be kept for at least 10 years after the product is out of production. They will be very valuable in the event of any product liability actions.

Quality of Content

The final comment on test documentation concerns quality of content. The documentation must include only relevant and objective information, data, facts, and results. Do not add any subjective statements, opinions, or unnecessary or irrelevant information. Doing so can be very damaging to your company in the event of any future product liability litigation. To emphasize this point with your organization, have your employees imagine trying to defend their documentation . . . in a court of law . . . while being interrogated by an aggressive lawyer . . . in front of television cameras . . . with their mother, spouse, and children at home . . . watching on television!

Enough said.

7

Supplier Quality Process
Verifying Process Performance

If you can't describe what you are doing as a process, you don't know what you're doing.

—W. Edwards Deming

S upplier quality process is about managing suppliers to verify error-prevention effectiveness and production process performance. The objective is to obtain maximum results with minimum effort while keeping primary ownership for quality with the factory making the product. This chapter is written from the perspective of supplier-manufactured product because so many companies now source their products from suppliers. The topics and concepts presented, however, apply to both in-house and sourced manufacturing.

The supplier quality process activities include the following:

1. Precontrol and positrol verification

2. Certifications

3. Error avoidance implementation

4. Performance metrics and trends

5. Management reviews

PRECONTROL AND POSITROL

Precontrol

Once a process has been determined to be capable of meeting the requirements (during product qualification), it is important to control the process during production to prevent the manufacture of defects. Controlling a process is simply charting the process output and taking the action indicated by the charted results. The action indicated by the chart will be to leave the process alone, adjust the process while it is running, or stop the process for adjustment and for another process capability verification (also called a requalification). The control chart alerts us to a change occurring in the process that requires an adjustment to prevent the process from making defective product.

Precontrol is the recommended process control method in terms of simplicity and power. It can be taught to an operator in 10 minutes, and it can help keep processes running hundreds of thousands and even millions of units without a single defect. The only requirement is that the process be capable at a Cpk of 1.33 or higher. This Cpk requirement must be verified during the process capability evaluation. Note that although a minimum Cpk of 1.33 is required for precontrol, one should really be using a Cpk of 2.0 or higher for product safety requirements.

Precontrol is described in four steps as follows.

Step 1: Set Up Precontrol Chart Zones

Divide the specification width by four to create the precontrol zones as shown in Figure 7.1. The zone created by the middle half of the specification width is designated as the green zone. The two zones on either side of the green zone are designated as the yellow zones. The two zones beyond the yellow zones are designated as the red zones.

Step 2: Qualify the Process

At process start-up, take five consecutive units from the process. If all five fall within the green zone, the process is qualified and production can begin. Proceed to step 3. However, if one or more of the units falls outside the green zone, the process is not qualified. The cause of the variation must be determined

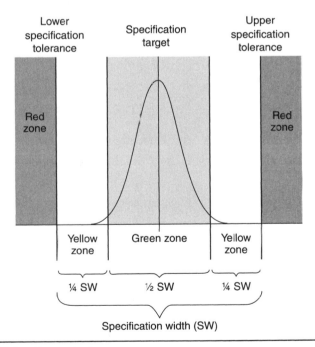

Figure 7.1 Precontrol zones.

and reduced or eliminated. After this is done, begin step 2 again to verify process qualification.

Step 3: Begin Precontrol Charting

After production begins, take two consecutive units from the process every half hour, record the results, and proceed according to the following rules:

1. If both units are in the green zone, continue production.

2. If one unit is in the green zone and the other is in the yellow zone, continue production.

3. If both units are in the same yellow zone, adjust the process while continuing to run production.

4. If each unit falls into a different yellow zone, stop production. The cause of variation must be determined and reduced or eliminated. After this is done, return to the beginning of step 2.

5. If one or both units are in the red zone, stop production. The cause of variation must be determined and reduced or eliminated. After this is done, return to the beginning of step 2.

Step 4: Adjust the Frequency of Precontrol Sampling

The frequency of sampling is adjusted based on dividing the average time period between two production stoppages by six. For example, if production was stopped because the two units were in opposite yellow zones and then stopped again six hours later because a unit was in the red zone, then the time period of six hours between stoppages is divided by six to give a sampling frequency of every hour. If the period between stoppages was six days, then the sampling frequency would be once a day.

Although you can certainly choose to increase the sampling frequency by applying a number larger than six in the denominator, it is not necessary in most applications. However, it is recommended that sampling occur at start-up after any process stoppage.

Positrol

Positrol is a tool used together with precontrol to ensure that important processing conditions are maintained at an optimum during production. The positrol chart identifies *what* processing parameters will be measured along with the specifications and tolerances, *who* will do the measuring, *how* and *where* the measurements will be taken, and *when* they will be taken.

For example, perhaps processing temperature and time are important in a drying process. The temperature (what) of the oven chamber entrance (where) is to be measured using a thermocouple potentiometer (how) by the laboratory technician (who) at the start of the shift (when). The specification is 350°F +/– 10°F. The drying time/conveyor belt speed (what) is to be measured using a stopwatch to measure drying cycle (how) by the laboratory technician (who) at the start of each shift (when).

The positrol chart, therefore, is just a who, what, how, where, and when log monitored by the process engineer or supervisor to ensure that optimum processing conditions are being maintained.

CERTIFICATIONS

Important elements of error prevention are education, training, and communication. These are also key ingredients of any certification process. In fact, a comprehensive certification process will keep you out of the wasteful product-inspection business and make your suppliers properly assume primary ownership for quality, cost, and delivery performance.

A comprehensive certification process begins with educating your suppliers on your product, process, and systems requirements applicable to the certification. This means your requirements and specification must be clearly defined and documented. The requirements then need to be reviewed with the supplier to make sure there is a full understanding. This review may include providing some education for the supplier. It may also include follow-up testing to ensure there is sufficient knowledge and understanding.

After the education process, there should be some follow-up training to ensure the supplier is properly applying the education and achieving the desired results. Once the supplier demonstrates this, the certification may be awarded.

The certification should be valid for a fixed period of time, perhaps one year. At the end of the certification period, a recertification should be required if both parties want to continue the business relationship.

There are different types of certification, for example, product certification, batch certification, personnel certification, process certification, and supplier certification. The most effective certifications, however, relate to the process (systems) or personnel, not to products or batches. *Remember: The process that creates the product determines product success or failure.*

Finally, it is important to perform routine supplier audits to verify continued supplier management and process performance. President Ronald Reagan said, "Trust, but verify." For our purposes here, it should be, "Educate, train, test, certify, and audit."

ERROR AVOIDANCE (POKA-YOKE)

Error avoidance means designing processes so that mistakes physically cannot happen. It means structuring the production process with constraints designed to prevent incorrect operation or operator mistakes. Error avoidance is also called poka-yoke, a Japanese term for the concept developed by Shigeo Shingo of Matsushita. In Japanese, *poka* means "inadvertent mistake" and *yoke* means "avoid."

Poka-yoke implementation can occur at any step of a manufacturing process where something can go wrong, but it is especially important where there are product safety concerns. Two examples from the toy industry will be presented: one on metal contamination prevention and one on paint batch control for ensuring paint compliance with toxicity requirements.

Example 1: Metal Contamination Prevention

The potential for hazardous metal contamination exists in certain products in the toy industry. For example, a concern with a sewn and stuffed rag doll is needles or needle fragments that appear in or on the doll. This contamination may not be discovered before the doll is packaged and shipped to the toy store. Even just one occurrence out of a million units sold is too many. It is therefore necessary to implement poka-yoke in the production process to prevent any and all hazardous metal contamination.

Poka-yoke begins with needle control at the sewing facility to prevent any loose needles or needle fragments from existing in the facility. Key elements of the needle control process are as follows:

1. All spare needles are kept locked in storage, and only the facility supervisor has the key.

2. In the event that a sewing machine needle breaks, the machine operator is required to gather all of the needle fragments and provide them to the supervisor. The supervisor will provide a new needle only when all of the broken needle fragments are found and returned.

3. If all of the needle fragments are not found, production stops and all product is quarantined and subject to metal detection until all needle fragments are found.

4. The supervisor tapes all needle fragments to the needle log and includes the date, time, machine, and operator information in the log. The log is kept inside the locked storage area.

This needle control procedure clearly helps prevent hazardous metal contamination, but it is not enough. There is also a need for metal contamination detection of the final packaged product.

To prevent accidents and inadvertent operator mistakes there are certain basic requirements for effective metal detection:

1. A conveyor type of metal detector that is capable of detecting very small, nonhazardous needle fragments must be used.

2. Two metal detectors must be used together in a series, and the product should be flipped and rotated before going through the second metal detector. This ensures that needle position in the doll will not be a factor in metal detection sensitivity. The redundancy also ensures an extremely high detection process reliability.

3. The pack-out area must be totally separate from the manufacturing area, and the only way for product to get from the manufacturing area to the pack-out area is through two metal detectors (see Figure 7.2). There is only a small opening in the wall, just large enough to accommodate the metal detector conveyor opening.

4. The metal detection room must be totally separate from both the manufacturing room and the pack-out room. The only way for product to get from the metal detection room to the pack-out room is through the second metal detector.

5. The metal detection machines are calibrated every hour or according to the calibration plan.

6. All metal detector rejects are kept in the metal detection room for analysis by product safety/quality engineering.

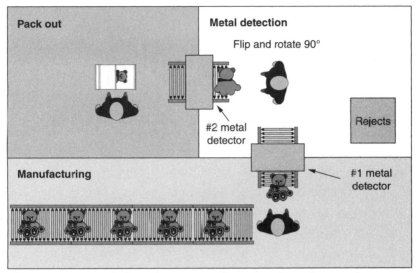

Figure 7.2   Metal detection process layout, orientation, and redundancy.

This type of metal detection process and procedure is an example of effective poka-yoke, or error avoidance. In fact, the metal contamination prevention and detection process is so effective that one would have to suspect sabotage somewhere in the supply chain in the event of a metal fragment complaint.

Example 2: Paint Batch Control

In the toy industry, painted products have strict requirements to ensure that they do not contain lead or other heavy element contamination. Any violation of these strict limits, no matter how low the contamination level, will result in a total product recall. It is therefore necessary to implement poka-yoke in the production process to prevent nonconforming paint violations. Key elements of paint batch control are as follows:

1. All paints are sourced only from approved paint supplier factories, and approved paint supplier factories do not manufacture any paints that are not approved for toy use.

2. The paint supplier tests every batch of paint for conformance to toy standards at a certified laboratory.

3. Every can of paint is labeled with the batch number, and it is not released to the toy manufacturing factory until the test report passes the paint batch. The test report is sent to the toy manufacturing factory.

4. When the toy factory receives the cans of paint from the paint supplier, all cans are immediately sent to a locked quarantine building. Every can is checked for batch number and batch test report. No cans are released to the factory unless they are labeled with a batch number with a passing test report.

5. Any can without a batch number label will be scrapped. Any can with a batch number with a failing test report will be scrapped. Any can with a batch number and without a test report will be held in quarantine.

6. When cans are emptied into smaller containers, such as touch-up dishes, the smaller containers must be identified with the original paint can batch number.

7. There is traceability of batch number to finished product date code.

Figure 7.3 depicts this paint batch control process. It is another example of effective poka-yoke. Without this level of process control, a company would be in jeopardy at some point of accidentally using nonconforming paints.

In summary, the purpose of poka-yoke is to eliminate product defects by preventing human errors. As the examples show, it is an effective and relatively inexpensive way of eliminating errors. The main objective of poka-yoke is to achieve zero defects. Poka-yoke implementation requires a thorough understanding and description of the process; otherwise, it will

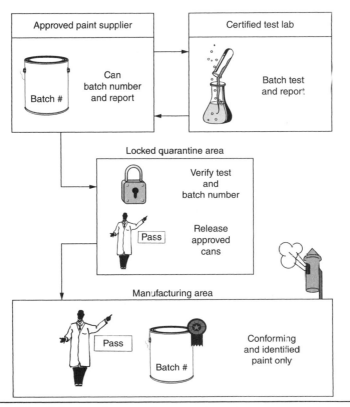

Figure 7.3 Paint batch control process layout.

not be successful. As Dr. Deming noted, if you can't describe what you are doing as a process, you don't know what you're doing.

PERFORMANCE METRICS AND TRENDS

The two most important performance metrics and trends for product safety purposes are total cost of quality and process average defective rate. Both product safety and product quality are concerned with preventing errors and defects, and these two metrics will best determine the safety and quality performance of a supplier.

Quality Costs

All quality costs can be grouped into one of four quality cost categories: prevention, appraisal, internal failure, and external failure. The total cost of quality is the sum of these four cost categories. Figure 7.4 lists the major components associated with each quality cost category.

The strategy must be to continually reduce the total cost of quality by investing resources in prevention. Resources are always scarce and precious, and they should not be wasted on appraisal or failure activities. A relatively small investment in prevention will yield a huge return in reduced failure costs, resulting in the desired reduction of total cost of quality. The best organizations spend the least on quality, and they accomplish this by investing in prevention.

Process Average Defective Rate

The amount of defective product produced, divided by the total amount of product produced (defective and nondefective) in a given time period, represents the average defective rate for that time period. As audits are performed on finished product from a production process, the audit results can be combined over a period of time to determine the average defective rate for the production process for that period of time. This is the process average defective rate, and it is an indication of how well the process is running and how well the prevention systems are working.

When all audits for a factory are combined, one gets a measure of that factory's process average defective rate, providing the audits are balanced with production activity so that the individual audit averages are properly weighted.

Trends

Measuring and tracking total cost of quality and defective rate trends is important for determining whether expected

1. **Prevention—"The Good"**

   Cost to prepare for an activity so it can be performed without error. Examples:
   - 1.1 Strategic and business planning for quality
   - 1.2 Developing quality requirements and specifications
   - 1.3 Developing quality measurements and goals
   - 1.4 Education and training
   - 1.5 Quality orientation
   - 1.6 Design reviews
   - 1.7 Product qualification
   - 1.8 New supplier quality evaluations
   - 1.9 Supplier quality seminars
   - 1.10 Process capability studies
   - 1.11 Process control
   - 1.12 Preventive maintenance

2. **Appraisal—"The Bad"**

   Cost related to inspecting an output to make sure it is error-free. Examples:
   - 2.1 Incoming, in-process, and final inspection and test
   - 2.2 Product quality audits
   - 2.3 Maintenance of inspection equipment
   - 2.4 Materials and supplies for inspection
   - 2.5 Processing and reporting on inspection data
   - 2.6 Evaluation of stock for degradation
   - 2.7 Status measurement and reporting
   - 2.8 Expense account reviews

3. **Internal failure—"The Ugly"**

   Cost when errors are detected before product is delivered to the customer. Examples:
   - 3.1 Scrap, including related labor, materials, and overhead
   - 3.2 Rework to correct defectives
   - 3.3 Reinspection of reworked products
   - 3.4 One hundred percent sorting inspection for defectives
   - 3.5 Engineering changes to correct a design error
   - 3.6 Manufacturing process changes to correct deficiencies
   - 3.7 Scrapping of obsolete product
   - 3.8 Difference between normal selling price and reduced price due to quality
   - 3.9 Unplanned downtime due to quality failures
   - 3.10 Inventory shrinkage
   - 3.11 Non-value-added activities

4. **External failure—"The Very Ugly"**

   Cost when errors are not detected before product is delivered to the customer. Examples:
   - 4.1 Defective returns
   - 4.2 Complaint handling
   - 4.3 Warranty charges
   - 4.4 Product recalls
   - 4.5 Product liability lawsuits
   - 4.6 Allowances made to customers due to substandard product
   - 4.7 Profit margin lost due to customer defection for quality

Figure 7.4 Total cost of quality categories.

improvement is occurring. Plotting both a 3-month moving average and a 12-month moving average will provide good information on current and longer-term trends. The supplier should keep this information available for periodic review by the manufacturer.

MANAGEMENT REVIEWS

Management reviews are periodic meetings that a manufacturer has with the management of a supplier to cover at least four basic agenda items:

1. Review performance and trends against goals

2. Follow up on implementation of past corrective action plans

3. Review any issues arising from quality systems audits

4. Establish any new corrective/preventive action plans

Management reviews may occur quarterly for new suppliers or suppliers with substandard performance. For suppliers that perform well, a formal management review may occur once per year.

It is important for suppliers to fully understand and appreciate the requirements and objectives of the manufacturer. When the manufacturer meets with the supplier to verify conformance to requirements and to review performance and progress against past corrective action plans, those requirements and action plans take on a whole new meaning. The management review meeting also provides an excellent opportunity for management to give positive feedback, praise good performance, and provide encouragement and support for any needed improvements noted in systems audit reports.

8

Strategic Auditing

Monitoring, Confirming, and Improving Effectiveness of Prevention Systems

You can observe a lot by just watching.

—YOGI BERRA

S trategic auditing is about accumulating information and knowledge for the purpose of improving the effectiveness of prevention systems. It is performed to measure supplier performance, to assess consumer complaints and returns, to analyze defects, and to build a product safety and quality knowledge database.

AUDITING SUPPLIER PERFORMANCE

If suppliers are properly operating in the prevention mode, then the only reason for auditing product is to verify that the prevention systems and processes are continuing to function correctly. Product auditing should not be performed to control material quality, product quality, or anything else.

Audits should be planned and performed to obtain an adequate amount of information with the minimum amount of effort and cost. Audits are only performed to ensure a reasonable level of confidence that the prevention systems are working. This type of auditing is called strategic auditing, and it is the only type of product auditing that should be planned, budgeted, and performed on suppliers.

It is important to note that confidence level in product auditing is almost totally dependent on the absolute size of the sample. It is practically independent of the total population or lot size from which the sample is taken. The sample size of the audit, therefore, should not be based on the lot size. And it should never be specified as a percentage of the lot size! Strategic audits should use small sample sizes and be frequent enough to ensure that the information will be representative over time. More frequent audits with small sample sizes is a better approach than infrequent audits with large sample sizes.

Strategic audits on suppliers' shipments are performed to develop a "report card" on each supplier's performance and to measure the effectiveness of each supplier's prevention process. The supplier's process average defective rate levels and trends should be tracked and reported. Again, small audit sample sizes with a planned periodic audit frequency should be used. Since product auditing is expensive, you only want to conduct just enough to obtain reasonable confidence on your performance and trend information. Any more auditing than that is a waste of time and money.

CONSUMER COMPLAINTS

Consumer complaints must be reviewed for any sign of a product safety issue. All product safety complaints must be reviewed by the product safety department, whether or not an injury occurred and whether or not they are real or only perceived safety issues. The review must begin immediately for at least two reasons:

1. Your consumers might be in jeopardy if the review reveals that an unreasonable risk of serious injury exists in one of your products. The product may need to be recalled.

2. The Consumer Product Safety Act (CPSA) section 15b requires immediate notification (within 24 hours) by the manufacturer once information is received that reasonably supports the conclusion that one of its products presents a substantial hazard, or presents an unreasonable risk of serious injury, or fails to comply with a CPSC regulation or rule. The CPSC allows a maximum of two weeks' time for investigation. Violations of section 15b can result in civil fines up to $15 million, not to mention possible criminal penalties.

When handling consumer complaints, there are certain things that should be done (Figure 8.1) and things that should not be done (Figure 8.2). Once a safety complaint has been completely

---

When handling a safety complaint, *do*:

1. Get name, address, phone number, and e-mail address of the complainant
2. Record what happened in the words of the complainant
3. Get details of any injury, including date, medical attention rendered, and missed work time
4. If no injury, get details of complainant's concern
5. Express regret for the unfortunate event or appreciation for the concern
6. Get product back for product safety evaluation
7. Compensate consumer with product and prepaid shipping label for product return
8. Thank the complainant for contacting you
9. Get Product Safety involved if complaint becomes too technical or difficult
10. Involve Legal/Risk Management if demand for monetary compensation is beyond product cost

Figure 8.1 Consumer safety complaint handling "do" list.

When handling a safety complaint, *do not*:

1. Admit any fault
2. Discuss any other complaints you might have had
3. Get angry or emotional
4. Offer opinions or draw any conclusions
5. Forget to document complaint and include in report to Product Safety and Legal/Risk Management
6. Forget to immediately notify Product Safety and Legal/Risk Management if there is a serious injury

---

Figure 8.2 Consumer safety complaint handling "do not" list.

resolved, the complaint information and resolution must be fully documented, kept on file, and evaluated for patterns and trends. At some point in the future, the CPSC may ask to see your complaint files. If you are ever in doubt about whether you should report a complaint to the CPSC, always err on the side of reporting it. There is really no disadvantage to reporting a complaint that might have been unnecessary to report. However, there can be consequences if you don't report the complaint and the CPSC later determines that it was necessary.

DEFECT ANALYSIS

When auditing supplier performance (defective rates), consumer complaints, and defective returns, the data need to be converted into information before they will be useful. You need to identify and isolate the vital few products and defects from the trivial many so that effective corrective action can be taken.

From the Pareto principle we know that approximately 20% or less of the product line contributes 80% or more of the complaints and returns. Further, we know that 20% or less of the root causes address 80% or more of the total effect (dollar loss). Therefore, your efforts should first be directed to only the top 20% of the products, and then to only the top 20% of the root causes for this top 20% of the products. This way the majority of the defect costs can be addressed while ignoring

80% of the products and also 80% of the defect causes for the remaining 20% of the products.

KNOWLEDGE DATABASE

The process of auditing factory performance, consumer complaints, and defective returns and analyzing defects and failures provides valuable information for improving the error-prevention tools and process. Just as the technical collaboration element provides important information at the beginning of the product development process, the strategic auditing element provides actual product and consumer experience information at the end of the process. This information provides a valuable opportunity to update and improve product safety tools such as the hazard and design review checklists and the product safety and reliability specifications.

The knowledge database, in a sense, becomes the brains of the entire prevention process. The many sources of information, from technical collaboration and regulatory standards to supplier audits and consumer complaints, continue to update and refresh the knowledge database (see Figure 8.3). This provides for improved error-prevention tools and a higher level of overall product integrity.

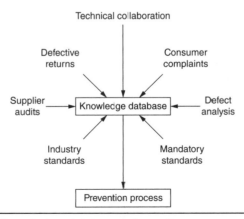

Figure 8.3 Knowledge database information sources.

CONVERTING DATA INTO WISDOM

The first step toward wisdom is to convert data into information. This is done by applying the Pareto principle to the data. The objective is to isolate the vital from the trivial. By isolating the vital few contributors and including this in the report, you convert the data into information. The report becomes user friendly and is much more likely to get management's attention and inspire action.

The second step is to convert information into knowledge. This is done by determining the vital few root causes for the variations or variances. By determining and reporting on the root causes, you can convert the information into knowledge. You achieve a higher level of understanding, and the report becomes more professional and actionable.

The third step is to convert knowledge into wisdom. This is done by implementing prevention systems to address the root causes of the variation or variances. When prevention systems are implemented to eliminate errors and variances, you will have achieved the highest level of understanding, called wisdom.

Figure 8.4 shows the progression from data to wisdom. The idea is to always seek a higher level of understanding. Strive to convert data into information, information into knowledge, and knowledge into wisdom.

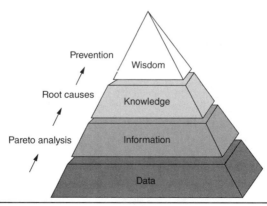

Figure 8.4   Hierarchy of understanding.

SUMMARY

Strategic auditing is about verifying that prevention systems are functioning correctly. It is about acquiring data and then converting those data into wisdom. It is essentially about watching supplier performance and consumer experiences with your product. As the great Yogi Berra said, "You can observe a lot by just watching."

9

Conclusion

Prevention is better than cure.

—Desiderius Erasmus

ERROR-PREVENTION PROCESS

Product safety excellence is achieved by addressing and eliminating any opportunities for safety errors at the earliest possible stage of product creation. This is accomplished with a prevention process of the seven vital elements (Figure 9.1).

Vital Element 1—Technical Collaboration

The process begins with the introduction of a new product concept. During the process of concept evaluation, technical collaboration begins with the network of technical experts and knowledge resources to ensure that the concept evaluation is thorough and any issues are immediately revealed.

Vital Element 2—Concept Evaluation

With the support of technical collaboration, the potential hazards can be identified, foreseeable use and misuse can be completely assessed, and human factors can be fully considered. This information is used to thoroughly evaluate and influence the product concept to ensure it is reasonably safe.

Vital Element 3—Design Qualification

Once the concept is fully evaluated and approved, the design qualification process begins. Note that technical collaboration may continue during design qualification. Design qualification occurs once design safety, reliability, and manufacturability have been confirmed.

Vital Element 4—Supplier Qualification

After design qualification, we move to product qualification. Before product qualification can occur, however, any new suppliers must be qualified. This is important because product qualification must occur with the testing of production-representative product samples from qualified suppliers. A supplier is qualified when its capabilities, capacities, controls, and management commitment are verified.

Vital Element 5—Product Qualification

Product qualification occurs when the product design, manufacturing, and testing conformance have been documented. When this happens the product is qualified for production start. This takes us to the supplier quality process.

Vital Element 6—Supplier Quality Process

The supplier quality process occurs during production of the product. It is verification that production controls are being maintained and that performance metrics and trends are acceptable.

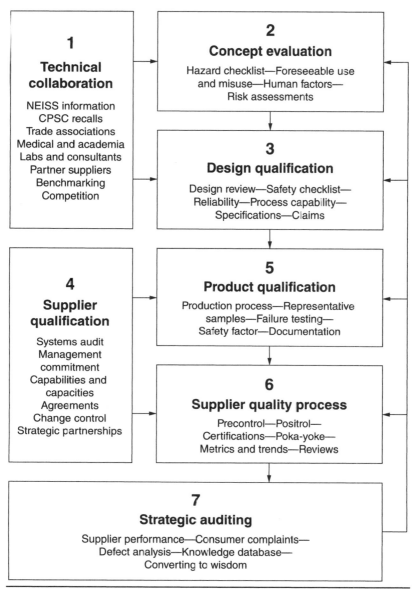

Figure 9.1 Product safety error-prevention process.

Vital Element 7—Strategic Auditing

The final element in the process is strategic auditing, where data from supplier performance and consumer experiences are converted into wisdom. Strategic auditing is about improving the effectiveness of the prevention system by continuing to update our checklists and specifications with new knowledge and wisdom. This knowledge and wisdom feed back into other major elements of our prevention process for continuous improvement.

The only way to achieve excellence in product safety is to prevent defects from occurring in the first place. Prevention means successfully applying appropriate tools and processes to eliminate opportunities for the occurrence of defects, errors, and waste. Figure 9.1 is a diagram of the product safety error-prevention system, showing the major tools and processes for each of the seven vital elements. The application of these seven elements will enable the achievement of product safety excellence. If, however, even one of the elements is missing or inadequate, success is jeopardized, and defects, waste, and product liability become significant problems.

PRODUCT LIABILITY PREVENTION

Product liability describes an action in which an injured party seeks to recover damages for harm from a seller or manufacturer when it is alleged that the harm resulted from a defective product. A product liability action, therefore, requires the establishment of a product defect. Without a product defect, there is no product liability.

Product defects can be design defects, manufacturing defects, or marketing (failure to warn) defects. Design defects exist when the product design presents an unreasonable risk of harm, no matter how well it was manufactured. Manufacturing defects exist when the product was manufactured with poor materials or workmanship. Failure-to-warn defects exist when the product has an inherent danger that is not obvious and that could be mitigated with adequate warnings, and the danger is present no matter how well the product is designed and manufactured.

The goal of product liability prevention, therefore, is to eliminate safety defects from the product. And the most effective way to eliminate defects is to prevent them from occurring in the first place. Prevention essentially means eliminating the opportunity for defects. As the Dutch scholar Desiderius Erasmus observed 500 years ago, prevention is better than cure.

PRODUCT SAFETY EXCELLENCE

As previously stated, there is no such thing as product safety perfection. There is no such thing as zero-hazard safety or zero-risk safety. These are concepts of perfection, and they are not expected or even possible in product safety.

At the other extreme, a product safety program that strives to meet only the minimum mandatory standards is inadequate. A product safety program that does not consider product reliability is inadequate. A product safety program that requires testing only to the specification is inadequate. These are concepts of deficiency, and they are not accepted or even suitable in product safety.

There is such a thing as product safety excellence, and it is not only possible but also desirable, essential, and vital. It is readily achievable using state-of-the-art knowledge and standards and a comprehensive error-prevention process. When all seven vital process elements are in place, product safety excellence will be achieved and maintained by your company. Product liability will be prevented and total quality costs will be substantially reduced. Consumer complaints and defective returns will be significantly reduced. Most importantly, you will earn the respect, trust, and loyalty of your consumers.

Best wishes on your journey to product safety excellence. Godspeed.

Appendix A

? ? Quiz ? ?

Twenty Questions to Test Your Product Safety Savvy

1. **Safety commitment**

   True or False

   The most important reason why safety goals are sometimes not achieved is because of insufficient commitment to safety.

2. **Definition**

   True or False

   Safety is defined as freedom from all risk.

3. **Primary goal**

   True or False

   The primary goal of a product safety function is to ensure that industry standards are met.

4. **Foreseeable use and misuse**

   True or False

   Products must be designed for all foreseeable consumer use and misuse.

5. **Conformance to requirements**

   True or False

   If the safety specification requires a product attachment to withstand a 21-pound pull force, and we test 10 product attachments to 21 pounds with no failure, we have demonstrated conformance to the safety requirement.

6. **State of the art**

   True or False

   Manufacturers are required to meet the state of the art with respect to product safety.

7. **Manufacturer responsibility**

   True or False

   Manufacturers are not responsible for a hazard that is scientifically unknowable at the time of manufacture.

8. **Reasonable risk**

   True or False

   Reasonable risk is a fact of life, and a reasonably safe product is not required to be an absolutely safe one.

9. **Intended use**

   True or False

   Intended use is established by the manufacturer's stated intent on the product or on the packaging.

10. Warnings

True or False

A warning about misuse for a product intended for ages six years and up will protect the manufacturer against product liability for that misuse.

11. Reliability

True or False

A safe product must be a reliable product.

12. Product safety changes

True or False

The best time for making product safety changes is at the concept evaluation stage of development.

13. Concept evaluation

True or False

When evaluating entirely new product concepts, the use of the hazard identification checklist, foreseeable use and misuse evaluation, and the human factors assessments will ensure a thorough and circumspect evaluation.

14. Process capability

True or False

A capable process must satisfy only two criteria:

1. The process is centered.

2. The process has acceptable variation.

15. **Product safety specification**

    True or False

    The product safety specification must be completed in time for production start so that production samples can be tested and released for shipment.

16. **Supplier evaluation**

    True or False

    The evaluation of a potential supplier must consider manufacturing capacities as well as manufacturing capabilities.

17. **Change control**

    True or False

    A change control policy is required to make sure that no changes occur during production.

18. **Factor of safety**

    True or False

    It is important that your internal safety standards be exactly the same as the federal regulatory safety standards.

19. **Poka-yoke**

    True or False

    Poka-yoke is a Japanese term for "error avoidance," and it means designing processes so that mistakes physically cannot happen.

20. **Strategic auditing**

    True or False

    Strategic auditing is primarily performed to control product quality.

Appendix B
!! Answers !!
to the Quiz

1. **Safety commitment:** The most important reason why safety goals are sometimes not achieved is because of insufficient commitment to safety.

   False. Achieving product safety excellence is more about comprehension than commitment. It requires an understanding and application of prevention tools and processes, such as hazard identification checklists, design risk analysis, factors of safety, reliability, process capability analysis, and process control. People are generally very committed to product safety but often unfamiliar with the right tools for achieving it.

   Reference: "Comprehension vs. Commitment" in Chapter 1.

2. **Definition:** Safety is defined as freedom from all risk.

   False. Safety is defined as freedom from *unacceptable* or *unreasonable* risk. Manufacturers are only required to ensure that their products are free from all unreasonable risks, not all risks.

   Reference: "Unreasonable Risk" in Chapter 1.

3. **Primary goal:** The primary goal of a product safety function is to ensure that industry standards are met.

   False. There are no industry standards that cover every possible product safety consideration. Although it is important and necessary to meet industry standards, it is almost always not sufficient.

   The primary goal is to protect the consumer against unreasonable risks of injury. An awareness and understanding of consumer injury data, reasonably foreseeable consumer use and misuse, and human factors are important considerations that must be included in a comprehensive product safety system.

   References: "Unreasonable Risk" and "Voluntary and Regulatory Requirements and Recalls" in Chapter 1.

4. **Foreseeable use and misuse:** Products must be designed for all foreseeable consumer use and misuse.

   False. Products need only be designed for all reasonably foreseeable consumer use and misuse. If product use that causes injury is not reasonably foreseeable, then no product liability exists.

   Reasonably foreseeable is generally defined as "what a reasonable person in the position of the defendant would have foreseen as a probable result." There are also regulations defining reasonably foreseeable use and abuse for certain specific situations.

   References: "Unreasonable Risk" in Chapter 1; "Foreseeable Use and Misuse" in Chapter 3.

5. **Conformance to requirements:** If the safety specification requires a product attachment to withstand a 21-pound pull force, and we test 10 product attachments to 21 pounds

with no failure, we have demonstrated conformance to the safety requirement.

False. If 10 units are tested to the specification and all pass, the best you can state is that you are 90% confident that the true failure rate is less than about 20% defective. This result would not be acceptable for product safety. The correct procedure is to test to failure and calculate the average test failure and the standard deviation. From these two parameters (mean and standard deviation) you can determine the failure rate in parts per million defective.

Reference: "Testing to Failure" in Chapter 6.

6. **State of the art:** Manufacturers are required to meet the state of the art with respect to product safety.

   True. Perfection is not possible for product safety, but product safety excellence is achieved when the state of the art is achieved. Anything less than state-of-the-art safety will put you in jeopardy of product liability losses.

   References: "State of the Art" in Chapter 1; "Product Safety Excellence" in Chapter 9.

7. **Manufacturer responsibility:** Manufacturers are not responsible for a hazard that is scientifically unknowable at the time of manufacture.

   True. As technology changes, new hazards emerge and it is not expected or even possible that they be addressed retroactively. It is, however, expected that manufacturers will meet the state-of-the-art technology and standards with respect to product safety.

   Reference: "Unreasonable Risk" in Chapter 1.

8. **Reasonable risk:** Reasonable risk is a fact of life, and a reasonably safe product is not required to be an absolutely safe one.

   True. Some considerations that can establish reasonable and acceptable risk are the following:

   — The availability of other, safer products

   — The obviousness of the risk or danger

   — Common knowledge and normal public expectation of the risk and danger

   — The usefulness and desirability of the product

   — The avoidability of injury by reasonable care in the use of the product

   Reference: "Unreasonable Risk" in Chapter 1.

9. **Intended use:** Intended use is established by the manufacturer's stated intent on the product or on the packaging.

   False. The manufacturer's stated intent is only one of several factors that must be considered to establish intended use. Other important factors that can outweigh stated intent are the product's advertising, promotion, and marketing, along with commonly recognized use of the product.

   Reference: "Intended Use and Product Labeling" in Chapter 3.

10. **Warnings:** A warning about misuse for a product intended for ages six years and up will protect the manufacturer against product liability for that misuse.

    False. The warning will offer no protection. It is reasonably foreseeable that a six-year-old child cannot and will not read and heed the warning. The product must not present unreasonable risks of injury during any reasonably foreseeable use and misuse.

    Reference: "Warning Label Problems" in Chapter 3.

11. **Reliability:** A safe product must be a reliable product.

    True. The product must remain safe during its lifetime. Reliability is an important part of product safety.

    Reference: "Reliability" in Chapter 4.

12. **Product safety changes:** The best time for making product safety changes is at the concept evaluation stage of development.

    True. The objective is to make the product inherently safe, and there is no better opportunity to do this than at concept evaluation, where changes are the easiest and least costly to implement.

    Reference: "Early Safety Influence" in Chapter 3.

13. **Concept evaluation:** When evaluating entirely new product concepts, the use of the hazard identification checklist, foreseeable use and misuse evaluation, and the human factors assessments will ensure a thorough and circumspect evaluation.

    False. Outside technical collaboration input is also generally required to ensure a complete and thorough evaluation.

    Reference: "Technical Collaboration Input" in Chapter 3.

14. **Process capability:** A capable process must satisfy only two criteria:

    1. The process is centered.
    2. The process has acceptable variation.

    False. A capable process must also be completely defined and documented.

    Reference: "Process Capability Analysis" in Chapter 4.

15. **Product safety specification:** The product safety specification must be completed in time for production start so that production samples can be tested and released for shipment.

    False. The safety and reliability specifications must be completed by the end of design qualification, because a qualified design must incorporate all safety concerns and requirements. It is also, therefore, immediately available for product qualification testing and approval, which occur before production start.

    Reference: "Safety Specification Development" in Chapter 4.

16. **Supplier evaluation:** The evaluation of a potential supplier must consider manufacturing capacities as well as manufacturing capabilities.

    True. Capacity is important because capacity issues often lead to capability issues. A supplier's attempts to fix capacity issues often lead to changes (processing time, substitute equipment, subcontracting, etc.) that result in quality and compliance issues.

    Reference: "Supplier Capabilities and Capacities" in Chapter 5.

17. **Change control:** A change control policy is required to make sure that no changes occur during production.

    False. A change control policy is required to ensure that no *unauthorized* changes occur during production. Unauthorized changes must be prevented so that product safety documentation is always current and valid. Change is not discouraged, because improvements occur through change. The change, however, must be qualified and authorized.

    Reference: "Change Control" in Chapter 5.

18. **Factor of safety:** It is important that your internal safety standards be exactly the same as the federal regulatory safety standards.

    False. It is important that your internal safety standards have a factor of safety significantly greater than 1.0 when compared with outside mandatory safety regulations. There is just too much variation affecting design, material, fabrication, testing equipment, and testing procedure to make your internal standards equal to the outside mandatory requirements.

    Reference: "Factor of Safety" in Chapter 6.

19. **Poka-yoke:** Poka-yoke is a Japanese term for "error avoidance," and it means designing processes so that mistakes physically cannot happen.

    True. Poka-yoke means structuring the production process with constraints designed to prevent incorrect operation or operator mistakes.

    Reference: "Error Avoidance (Poka-Yoke)" in Chapter 7.

20. **Strategic auditing:** Strategic auditing is primarily performed to control product quality.

    False. Strategic auditing is performed to verify that prevention systems are working effectively and to monitor supplier performance trends.

    Reference: "Auditing Supplier Performance" in Chapter 8.

Index

Belong to the Quality Community!

Established in 1946, ASQ is a global community of quality experts in all fields and industries. ASQ is dedicated to the promotion and advancement of quality tools, principles, and practices in the workplace and in the community.

The Society also serves as an advocate for quality. Its members have informed and advised the U.S. Congress, government agencies, state legislatures, and other groups and individuals worldwide on quality-related topics.

Vision

By making quality a global priority, an organizational imperative, and a personal ethic, ASQ becomes the community of choice for everyone who seeks quality technology, concepts, or tools to improve themselves and their world.

ASQ is...

- More than 90,000 individuals and 700 companies in more than 100 countries
- The world's largest organization dedicated to promoting quality
- A community of professionals striving to bring quality to their work and their lives
- The administrator of the Malcolm Baldrige National Quality Award
- A supporter of quality in all sectors including manufacturing, service, healthcare, government, and education
- YOU

Visit www.asq.org for more information.

ASQ Membership

Research shows that people who join associations experience increased job satisfaction, earn more, and are generally happier*. ASQ membership can help you achieve this while providing the tools you need to be successful in your industry and to distinguish yourself from your competition. So why wouldn't you want to be a part of ASQ?

Networking

Have the opportunity to meet, communicate, and collaborate with your peers within the quality community through conferences and local ASQ section meetings, ASQ forums or divisions, ASQ Communities of Quality discussion boards, and more.

Professional Development

Access a wide variety of professional development tools such as books, training, and certifications at a discounted price. Also, ASQ certifications and the ASQ Career Center help enhance your quality knowledge and take your career to the next level.

Solutions

Find answers to all your quality problems, big and small, with ASQ's Knowledge Center, mentoring program, various e-newsletters, *Quality Progress* magazine, and industry-specific products.

Access to Information

Learn classic and current quality principles and theories in ASQ's Quality Information Center (QIC), *ASQ Weekly* e-newsletter, and product offerings.

Advocacy Programs

ASQ helps create a better community, government, and world through initiatives that include social responsibility, Washington advocacy, and Community Good Works.

Visit www.asq.org/membership for more information on ASQ membership.

*2008, The William E. Smith Institute for Association Research

ASQ Certification

ASQ certification is formal recognition by ASQ that an individual has demonstrated a proficiency within, and comprehension of, a specified body of knowledge at a point in time. Nearly 150,000 certifications have been issued. ASQ has members in more than 100 countries, in all industries, and in all cultures. ASQ certification is internationally accepted and recognized.

Benefits to the Individual

- New skills gained and proficiency upgraded
- Investment in your career
- Mark of technical excellence
- Assurance that you are current with emerging technologies
- Discriminator in the marketplace
- Certified professionals earn more than their uncertified counterparts
- Certification is endorsed by more than 125 companies

Benefits to the Organization

- Investment in the company's future
- Certified individuals can perfect and share new techniques in the workplace
- Certified staff are knowledgeable and able to assure product and service quality

Quality is a global concept. It spans borders, cultures, and languages. No matter what country your customers live in or what language they speak, they demand quality products and services. You and your organization also benefit from quality tools and practices. Acquire the knowledge to position yourself and your organization ahead of your competition.

Certifications Include
- Biomedical Auditor – CBA
- Calibration Technician – CCT
- HACCP Auditor – CHA
- Pharmaceutical GMP Professional – CPGP
- Quality Inspector – CQI
- Quality Auditor – CQA
- Quality Engineer – CQE
- Quality Improvement Associate – CQIA
- Quality Technician – CQT
- Quality Process Analyst – CQPA
- Reliability Engineer – CRE
- Six Sigma Black Belt – CSSBB
- Six Sigma Green Belt – CSSGB
- Software Quality Engineer – CSQE
- Manager of Quality/Organizational Excellence – CMQ/OE

Visit www.asq.org/certification to apply today!

ASQ Training

Classroom-based Training

ASQ offers training in a traditional classroom setting on a variety of topics. Our instructors are quality experts and lead courses that range from one day to four weeks, in several different cities. Classroom-based training is designed to improve quality and your organization's bottom line. Benefit from quality experts; from comprehensive, cutting-edge information; and from peers eager to share their experiences.

Web-based Training

Virtual Courses

ASQ's virtual courses provide the same expert instructors, course materials, interaction with other students, and ability to earn CEUs and RUs as our classroom-based training, without the hassle and expenses of travel. Learn in the comfort of your own home or workplace. All you need is a computer with Internet access and a telephone.

Self-paced Online Programs

These online programs allow you to work at your own pace while obtaining the quality knowledge you need. Access them whenever it is convenient for you, accommodating your schedule.

Some Training Topics Include
- Auditing
- Basic Quality
- Engineering
- Education
- Healthcare
- Government
- Food Safety
- ISO
- Leadership
- Lean
- Quality Management
- Reliability
- Six Sigma
- Social Responsibility

Visit www.asq.org/training for more information.